CLASSIC GUNS OF THE WORLD SERIES

GERMAN SUBMACHINE GUNS
1918–1945

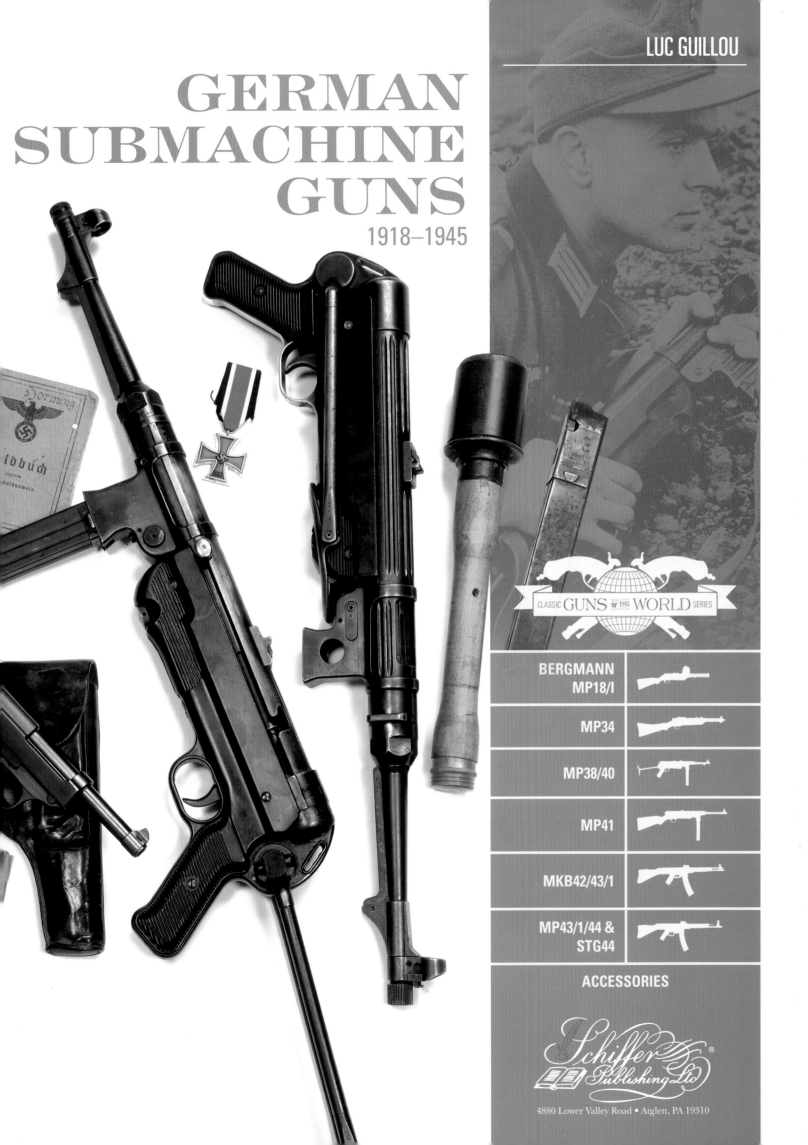

LUC GUILLOU

GERMAN SUBMACHINE GUNS
1918–1945

CLASSIC GUNS OF THE WORLD SERIES

BERGMANN MP18/I	
MP34	
MP38/40	
MP41	
MKB42/43/1	
MP43/1/44 & STG44	
ACCESSORIES	

Schiffer Publishing Ltd

4880 Lower Valley Road • Atglen, PA 19310

CONTENTS

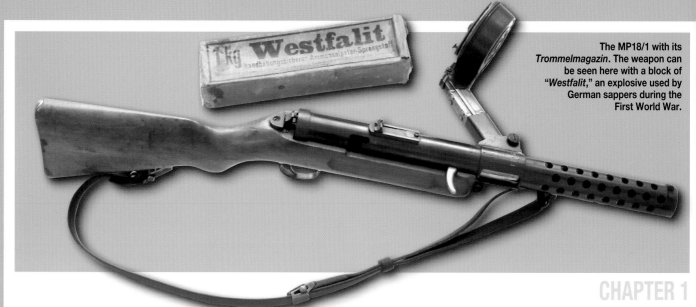

The MP18/1 with its *Trommelmagazin*. The weapon can be seen here with a block of "*Westfalit*," an explosive used by German sappers during the First World War.

CHAPTER 1

THE BERGMANN MP 18/1

The use of the Villar-Perosa by the Italians incited the Austrians to adapt certain Steyr pistols to fire in continuous burst fire: here is a Steyr 1912 model modified in 1916, equipped with a fire mode selector and a lengthened magazine. This pistol, provided with a fixed 16-round magazine and not with a removable magazine, had to be reloaded with 8-round magazine clips that rendered it rather ineffective.

From the eve of the First World War, the German army had planned to equip some of its combatants with rapid fire weapons. It was in this context that a long barreled version of a P.08 pistol was adopted: the LP08, on which it was possible to mount a short wooden stock and which could be fed by a 32-round drum magazine.

This long Luger was destined to be assigned to members of artillery and machine gun batteries to offer them a compact weapon enabling them to ensure a close defense of their equipment. In the same spirit, the Mauser C.96 pistol, equipped with a stock holster, could also be used as a small semi-automatic carbine to ensure a close defense role.

In the middle of the war, the Germans, on the initiative of *General* Oskar von Hutier set up "*Stoßtruppen*" also called "assault troops," whose men, armed principally with carbines, pistols, and grenades had the mission of infiltrating enemy lines in order to disorganize the defenses.

It quickly became clear that, for this type of action, a weapon that was both compact and capable of continuous burst fire could bring a clear advantage.

Infantry equipment: pistols, rifles, and machine guns did not respond in all types of close-combat situations where it was necessary to saturate the enemy target with bullets. The first two weapons did not have enough firepower and the third, even in its lighter version (model 08/15) was not mobile enough to accompany troops during attacks on enemy positions.

The Allies found the answer by putting into service light machine guns such as the British Lewis, the French Chauchat, or the American BAR.

These weapons, capable of being transported and put into operation by a single man, meant that situations such as those mentioned above could be confronted provided that they were supplied in large enough quantities.

At the end of the war, American troops brought another type of response to this challenge by providing "pump" action hunting rifles: the famous "Trench guns," firing 12-caliber buckshot cartridges which simultaneously sent seven to nine bullets of 8 mm caliber on the target.

The superb semi-automatic Mauser and Mondragon carbines that the Germans had in small quantities did not respond well to the demands of close combat. These weapons fired a rifle cartridge too powerful to allow a continuous burst fire version to be developed. In addition they were too costly to make in large quantities and also their complex mechanism was too delicate to withstand the mud of the trenches. These mechanical wonders were consequently reserved for aviation.

After the First World War all European nations carefully examined the weapons retrieved from the battlefields. This excellent photo, published in *Life* magazine in 1938, shows two Czechoslovakian officers at the firing range trying out two 18/1 submachine guns. The photo also shows a box of fifty Geco oil resistant cartridges (Oeldicht) and an open P. Kasten and two pistols: one a Walther PP.

A group of Austro-Hungarian officers, including the crown prince, watches the presentation of a Villar-Perosa taken from the Italian army.

Grip on a Villar-Perosa: triggers with grid-patterns can be seen on both sides. In the absence of modifications, both hands are needed to use the weapon with this configuration.

Theodor Bergmann, German industrialist and pioneer of the automatic pistol, who made the submachine gun Bergmann 18 in his factory in Gagenau and whose name subsequently remained attached to the weapon.

The first response to this need of a light weapon with good fire power that the central powers explored consisted of transforming semi-automatic pistols to render them capable of firing in bursts. We know of LP 08 and C.96 modified in such a way (and sometimes even done so by their users!).

For their part the Austrians transformed some Steyr 1912 pistols to fire automatically. But the lightness and high firing rate of such weapons made them very difficult to control during bursts of fire. Besides, their small magazine capacity exposed their users to being faced with a prematurely empty magazine before being able to neutralize their objective!

An Italian Invention

It seems it was the Italians who started, doubtless unwittingly, the evolution which led to the concept of a submachine gun in adopting in 1915 an double barrel, ultra-light submachine gun conceived by the famous Italian weapons inventor Abiel Revelli and made by the Villar-Perosa establishment. The Villar-Perosa 1915 model fired 9 mm cartridges from the Glisenti 1910 model and was fed by detachable 25-round magazines. This weapon had been designed to be used as a machine gun to assist the infantry but also as an aviation weapon at a time when low engine power limited the load that planes could carry.

The Villar-Perosa resembles the SIA (Societa Italiana Anonima G. Ansaldo Armstrog i co) machine gun conceived by G. Agnelli where the opening of the non-fixed breech was delayed by a rotation movement prior to the opening.

Unlike the SIA machine gun, which fired a rifle cartridge, the Villar-Perosa was chambered for the 9 mm Glisenti pistol cartridge, whose power was slightly less than that of the 9 mm German Parabellum.

The use of a pistol cartridge had the advantage of facilitating the operation of the non-fixed breech but it limited the efficiency of the Villar-Perosa as a support weapon to a practical range of 200 meters. In addition the Villar-Perosa had an excessive rate of fire (in the order of 1,200 shots per minute for each barrel) which made it difficult to control during firing unless it was mounted on a heavy carriage but the use of which cancelled out all the advantages of compactness and the relative lightness (8 kg) of the weapon.

The Hugo Schmeisser Submachine Gun

It was finally in Germany that the veritable submachine gun was born following the launch of a program by the German army from 1916 for the development of a short carbine capable of continuous burst fire of P.08 pistol cartridges and fed by a drum magazine already in service on the LP08.

The study of this weapon was entrusted by the light weapons testing commission (*Gewehr Prüfungs Kommission* or G.P.K.) to the Bergmann company in 1917.

The development of this weapon called "*Maschinen-pistol*" was led by the engineer Hugo Schmeisser. Schmeisser was employed by the Bergmann company of Suhl, whose founder Theodor Bergmann had been a major advocate of the development of the automatic pistol.

The drum-magazine lips go deeply into the receiver and prevent the breech from closing when necessary.

The 1915 model Villar-Perosa. This weapon fired pistol ammunition whose weak fire power meant a non-fixed breech operation was possible, with a simple opening delay engendered by a rotation of the breech. It was a downsized version of the Italian SIA machine gun.

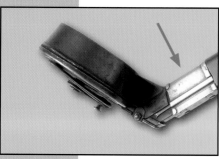

When the "*Trommelmagazin*" (drum magazine) was used on an MP18/I, a block had to be placed on the straight part to prevent it from penetrating too far in the magazine housing under the effect of an impact from the left side.

Famous photo taken in Berlin in 1918 showing a policeman armed with an MP18/I. The man also has a drum magazine tucked under his belt, along with a holster for a 15 cm barreled Marine Luger.

Collectors still ask the question today how Bergmann became so inspired from examining a Villar-Perosa machine gun captured by the Austrians on the Italian front.

It would have been normal for a weapons designer, working during war-time on an urgent military program to have been given the opportunity of examining a captured enemy weapon as a part of his research.

However, even though the Bergmann submachine gun takes up the principle of using a pistol cartridge, its operating system and its design are totally different from those of the Italian light machine gun.

The weapon conceived by Hugo Schmeisser and made by the Bergmann establishment started to be used by the German army the following year under the name MP18-1 (or MP18/I).

The suffix "-1" or "/I" can be interpreted in one of two ways:

- either it indicates a detail modification brought to the originally adopted model at the request of the army,

- or the German army had been offered several listed prototypes "MP18-I," "MP18-2," "MP18-3" and so on and it was the "18-1" which was retained and the name was kept.

As soon as the GPK had recommended the adoption of the MP18/I, the war ministry placed an order of 50,000 weapons with the Bergmann establishment. Bergmann was only able to deliver approximately 10,000 before the armistice of November 1918. The manufacture continued after the armistice, meaning a total of around 45,000 MP18/Is were able to be delivered.

The choice of the name MP "*Maschinenpistole*" showed that the general staff of the German army immediately had a clear vision of the tactical use that it intended to attribute to this weapon; a type of pistol fitted with a butt and with great firepower.

Between the wars many other armies were to lose their way with confused conceptions by assigning these weapons, which fired pistol cartridges, the role of support weapon and this explains the name sub machine gun for the Americans, "*mitraillette*" for the French, and "*sub-fucil*" for the Spanish.

The British and Italians presented a different concept, who saw an automatic carbine capable of firing in bursts if necessary in the PM ("Machine carbine" for the British and "Moschetto automatic" for the Italians): a concept which heralded the assault rifle.

The MP18/I entered service in the German army during the first months of 1918. It was planned to allocate around six submachine guns per company where these weapons had to be used by a two-man team made up of a shooter and an ammunition server transporting several magazines.

German soldier armed with an MP18/I photographed in France in 1918.

Cloth bag used for transporting the drum magazine from the belt. This piece of kit was used by ammunition servers accompanying shooters of the MP18/I. *Photo by Marc de Fromont*

For close combat, the MP18/I replaced the Mauser C.96 and P.08 pistols seen above.
Above the weapon: the 32-round drum magazine and a 1917 model stick grenade.
Below: a second class iron cross and a "Gibraltar" armband, assigned to certain
Hanoverian regiments in commemoration of the help that they brought to British
troops before the French revolution to defend the famous rock against the French.
Collection of the Royal Army Museum of Brussels, photo by Marc de Fromont

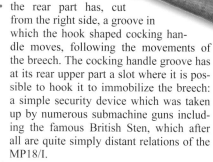

MP18/I transformed by the Finnish army to a selective fire weapon by the fitting of a trigger for single shot fire. *BWB Koblenz*

Marking "1920" on the butt of an MP18 used by the army or the police of the Weimar Republic. This marking meant weapons could be identified and recorded in the inventories of the *Reichswehr* and the police force. It indicated that they were used in an official capacity by the state and not clandestine weapons of which there were many in Germany at that time.

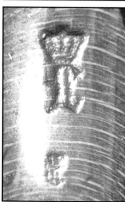

Acceptance stamps on the butt of two MP18/I

A member of the German rail police (*Bahnschutz*) practicing firing an MP18/I. It can be noted that he is holding the weapon by its magazine; not a recommended method of firing as it could lead to feeding incidents.

Carts derived from those used for MG08/15 light machine guns were used to transport magazines and spare ammunition, contained in boxes called "P. Kasten," as near as possible to the front lines.

Presentation

Apart from the magazine, which is made from pressed sheet metal, the metal parts of the MP18/I are machined in a traditional way. However, no part has a truly complex form, which renders the manufacture of the MP18/I both simple and inexpensive.

The MP18/I resembles a short carbine, fitted with a butt in beech wood keeping the half pistol grip butt of Mauser 1898 model Mauser rifles and carbines, on which a cylindrical receiver is mounted bearing two parts:

- the forward part, composed of a tube perforated with circular cooling holes which allow air to circulate around the barrel to keep it cool and also enable the weapon to be held without the shooter running the risk of burning his hand on the barrel. This cooling jacket houses a 20 cm long barrel and is chambered for a 9 mm Parabellum cartridge. The case has a triangular foresight mounted on a dovetail at its forward part. This foresight prevented the unscrewing of the disc joined to the front of the barrel. To disassemble the barrel it is necessary therefore to remove the foresight beforehand and then unscrew the barrel and remove it from the case from the front.

- the rear part has, cut from the right side, a groove in which the hook shaped cocking handle moves, following the movements of the breech. The cocking handle groove has at its rear upper part a slot where it is possible to hook it to immobilize the breech: a simple security device which was taken up by numerous submachine guns including the famous British Sten, which after all are quite simply distant relations of the MP18/I.

This rear section also has on its upper part a sight with two leaves mounted at right angles and with the sighting notches calibrated for distances of 100 and 200 meters. This choice of distance well confirms how the submachine guns were used by the German army.

The trigger mechanism, fixed to the lower part of the receiver, is designed only for continuous burst fire.

The rear of the receiver is closed by a cap connected by continuous threads. The cap has a lever which ensures the receiver is locked on the frame of the weapon.

The buffer pitot of the recoil spring is fixed to the front part of the breech cover.

The rear part of the receiver contains a cylindrical breech at the rear of which a mobile firing pin is embedded, inside which a small diameter recoil spring is housed.

The open and non-fixed breech firing system of the MP was conceived by Hugo Schmeisser in order that the percussion takes place slightly before the breech closes completely. Because of this, the cartridge case in the chamber starts to move backwards before the breech has finished its forward movement.

This rear movement of the case tends to push the breech back to the rear.

This short phase during which the movement of the case and that of the breech are in opposition contributes to slow the firing rate (around 500 shots per minute), which diminishes recoil and the elevation of the weapon: this is the principle that American authors christened API or Advanced Primer Ignition.

The Drum Magazine

Between the forward and rear parts of the receiver there is a central magazine housing block which has an ejection port on its right and on the left a magazine housing inclined at a 45° angle towards the rear, in which the 32-round drum magazine developed for the LP08 is positioned.

This magazine was the main defect of the MP18/I, as it was costly to make, delicate to load, and fragile yet bulky. A second defect was the small diameter of its recoil spring.

The Bergmann company had already developed straight, double-stack double-feed cartridges for some of its automatic pistols.

Reconstruction of the interior of a P. Kasten. *Georges Machtelinckx*

Surprising photo of a soldier of the *Wehrmacht* still armed with an MP18/I. The use of the MP18/I, non-modified for the use of a straight magazine, seems to have been relatively rare at this time.

The examination of a captured Villar-Perosa would have also enabled them to use the excellent Revelli magazine system mounted on this weapon as a source of inspiration; this had two columns of interlocking cartridges which presented alternatively in the lips of the magazine.

To equip the MP18/I with an anachronistic drum magazine used with the LP 08 certainly originated in a demand made by the German general staff of not multiplying the number of magazines in service.

This desire to standardize equipment was fully understandable in the context of the great shortages that Germany was enduring in 1918.

Despite its older magazine, the MP18/I was compact, easy to use, and inexpensive to produce.

This ease of manufacture meant the weapon could be produced quickly and distributed to the assault troops (*Stoßtruppen*) engaged in the Ludendorff Offensive in the summer of 1918.

The simplicity of the weapon also meant that the weapon could be used on a large scale. At the end of the war, the German army envisaged to equip all officers and non-commissioned officers with the weapon along with ten percent of men in the ranks. Ammunition and spare magazines had to be transported in small carioles in the order of one cariole for two MPs.

Just as there were machine gun companies within German regiments, it was planned to create sections of six "machine gunners" aided by six submachine gunners per company. The end of the war brought this project to an end.

The manufacture of the MP18/I continued by Bergmann during 1919 and 1920 before the Treaty of Versailles (decreed on January 10, 1920) broke up the German weapon industry and forbad the manufacture of weapons of war in Germany.

In the *Reichswehr*

The *Reichswehr* decided to provide six submachine guns per company. These weapons were proof stamped with the mark "1920" indicating they belonged to the army of 100,000 men that the Treaty of Versailles had conceded to a defeated Germany.

The Allied inspection commission for German disarmament was troubled by the number of MPs supplied by the *Reichswehr* and reprimanded the German authorities, who then ordered the MPs be transferred to the police.

In fact, even though the number of machine guns held by the army had been severely limited by the Allies, clauses in the Treaty of Versailles had omitted to specify the authorized number of MPs along with the number of the police force.

This oversight enabled the German government to camouflage the numbers easily available. In this period of economic crisis, there were many volunteers to serve in the police force. The police could therefore engage trained soldiers as a preference, those who had experience of firing in a military context, under the guise of standard police or anti-riot forces. These police forces were allocated substantial armaments. Every uniformed policeman was personally equipped with a P.08 pistol and three magazines, a carbine, and a bayonet. In addition, police stations and commissioners held automatic weapons (MP18/I and MG08/15) in their armories. In the event of the resurgence of revolutionary discord that had brought bloodshed to the country in 1918 and 1919, the forces of order would therefore be well-equipped to deal with this.

The Allies, not wanting to see Germany swing towards communism, closed their eyes to this arrangement.

The MP18/I had been used with effectiveness in street combat by the units that had broken the Spartacist revolutionary movement. The equipment list of the famous *Rossbach Freikorps* had no fewer than 92 MP18/I weapons.

Between the wars, the MP18/I was therefore essentially used as a police weapon. This state of affairs, coupled with the brevity of its military use during the last months of the war, subsequently led to many foreign armies to detract from the military angle of this weapon and focus more on the law enforcement aspect.

The P. Kasten: transport case for MP18/I drum magazines, contains five drum magazines and thirty-two boxes of sixteen reserve cartridges (enough to load sixteen magazines) along with a tool for loading the magazines. *Georges Machtelinckx*

CHAPTER 2

THE MODIFIED MP 18/1

The modified MP18/I is distinguishable from the original model by the replacement of its magazine housing with another made by Haenel, following a Schmeisser patent, which enabled the use of straight magazines, much less bulky than the drum magazines used originally.

During the French campaign in 1940, a German motorcyclist takes aim from a comrade's shoulder for precise shooting with his modified MP18/I. This is very likely a posed photo because the comrade would certainly not have appreciated having shell cases ejected directly towards his face!

The name of the manufacturer is stamped on the forward part of the magazine housing.

Marking on a modified MP18/I : the surname of the inventor, Hugo Schmeisser, is stamped on the magazine housing

Marking on the side of the barrel.

THEODOR BERGMANN ABT. WAFFENBAU SUHL

The Treaty of Versailles had banned the German army from holding pistols with a barrel longer than 10 cm, consequently many LP08 were destroyed or modified by having their barrel shortened.

In this context, the already uncertain concept of a pistol that was transformable to a small automatic carbine lost all justification, and the butts, as well as the drum magazines designed for the LP08, became useless and were destroyed in great number.

There was no longer any reason therefore to conserve, for the sake of standardization of equipment, the 32-round drum-magazine, which destabilized the weapon and was detrimental to its reliability.

During the 1920s, the engineer Hugo Schmeisser suggested a modification to the weapon meaning it could be fed with a straight magazine with two interlocking columns of cartridges which came together in a central position at the lips of the magazine.

The patent for this modification, which included the replacement of the magazine housing of the MP18/I, was bought by the Hamel company of Suhl where Hugo Schmeisser had the role of technical director.

Progressively the MP18/I remaining in service benefitted from this modification, and this explains why the non-modified MP18/I have today become quite rare.

Some modified MP18/Is used by the police were equipped with a supplementary safety system: the "safety block" (*Blocksicherung*): a part which, when rotated, blocked the breech in a forward position and prevented accidental rear movement, a typical cause of accidents on the MP.

In 1939, all the available modified MP18/Is were requisitioned by the *Wehrmacht*.

User manual for a modified MP18/I published under the Weimar Republic.

The photos of the French campaign of 1940 show combatants equipped more often with modified MP18/I rather than MP38 or 40, still relatively uncommon at that time, and supplied as a priority to armored units and parachutists.

The MPs Derived from the Bergmann MP18/I

If the victors of 1918 concentrated their interest on certain German weapons (combat gas, submarines, airships, machine guns), whose destructive effects they

Modified and non-modified MP18/l surrounded
by several objects of the Weimar Republic and
Freikorps. Collection of the Royal Army Museum
of Brussels, photo by Marc de Fromont

SIG 1920 model: a very close variation of the modified MP18/I, distinguishable by its straight bolt handle, its markings, and its tangential sight. *Mauser*

Comparison between the magazine housing of an MP18/I in its original state (left) and a modified MP18/I (right).

Chinese submachine gun which took inspiration from the MP28/II developed with the cooperation of Heinrich Vollmer by the Tsing Dao metalworks. This weapon even though very close to the Bermann is marked Vollmer submachine gun.

had experienced, their technical services nonetheless tested the MP18/I s that came into their hands. But the three major players in the victory of 1918 (France, United Kingdom, and the USA) having opted to organize their groups around a submachine gun, meant smaller armies would model themselves on this choice.

The MP18/I was however produced in a limited number in two countries: Switzerland and Estonia.

Switzerland: The MPSIG 1920

The production of the weapon began again in Switzerland as the manufacture of submachine guns was forbidden in a defeated Germany from 1920.

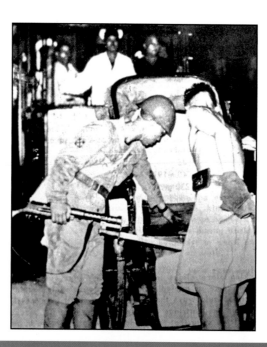

Japanese marines carrying out identity checks in Tiensin in 1939. The man in the foreground is armed with SIG 1920 fitted with a part allowing an Arisaka rifle bayonet to be fitted. *Thomas B. Nelson*

The manufacture of a copy of the modified MP18/I was organized by the Swiss Industrial Company (SIG), who ensured, completely legally, the exportation to conflict zones in the period between the two world wars (in particular Finland, Latin America, and China).

The SIG 1920 was also bought by Japan in 7.63 mm Mauser caliber where it was used by the marines. The Japanese version was fitted with a system allowing the fixing of an Arisaka rifle bayonet. In 1940, Japan put into service a nationally made submachine gun called "type 100" and chambered for 8 mm Nambu.

Estonia: The Tallin Submachine Gun

Estonia also manufactured, in the Tallin arsenal around 1923, a copy of the MP18/I in 9 mm Parabellum caliber. This fairly rare weapon was exported to Spain during the civil war (as indeed were many other types of weapons).

The Tallin conserved a small diameter recoil spring similar to that of the MP18/I but different from the German weapon by its bolt handle ending in a curved form, by the oblong shape of its openings on the cooling jacket, and by the presence of a fire mode selector fixed at the rear and bringing to mind the future MP28.

China

Between the two world wars, China was a very great consumer of weapons of all types, because of particularly tragic events that took place during that period and tied to three factors:

- combats conducted against the central power by regional despots called "war lords."

- combats between communists and nationalists.

- the Japanese invasion which started by Japanese troops entering Manchuria in 1937 and only ended with the defeat of Japan in 1945.

Haenel marking on the magazine of a modified MP18/I, also bearing the stamp PTV (*Polizei Teschnische Verwaltung*) the technical service of the police.

Marking of the *Schutzpolizei* of Schleswig.

Another less common variation of the MP18/I: the Estonian Tallin several examples of which were used during the Spanish civil war. *Mauser*

From top to bottom: MP28 and MP18 magazines for 50, 32, and 20 rounds. The 50-round magazine is intended for the Finnish 1920 SIG. Just a question of a few tenths of a millimeter meant that the MP18/I and MP28/II magazines were not interchangeable: the straight MP18/I magazines go into the MP28/II magazine housing but not the reverse.

Chinese soldier photographed in 1937. He is armed with a SIG 1920 and equipped with a chest magazine pouch containing a pocket for a loading tool. *Thomas B. Nelson*

The various factions involved imported just about all types of submachine guns and automatic pistols with a continuous burst fire capability available on the market at that time. The western powers had the honest intention of bringing peace by imposing an embargo on weapons exports to China, but the involved parties had copies of western weapons made by the arsenals that they controlled.

It seems that the German engineer Heinrich Vollmer carried out a trip to China to set up the manufacture of his conception of a submachine gun based on the Bergmann at the Tsing Dao arsenal.

Police magazine pouch for three 20-round magazines.

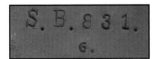

Berlin police markings ("S.B." for *Schutzpolizei Berlin*) on a modified MP18/I magazine.

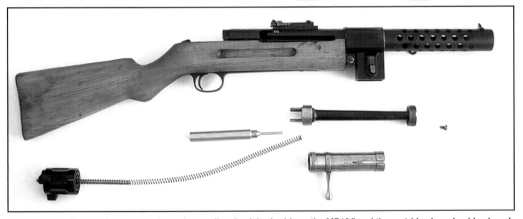

Disassembled Chinese Schmeisser. Note the recoil spring inherited from the MP18/I and the cartridge barrel guide placed at the rear of the barrel, are also on the SIG 1920 and the MP35/I.

Weapon marking: the rough translation is 7.63 caliber, Tsing Dao metalworks, year No.10 of the Republic (1927).

THE MP28/II SUBMACHINE GUN

A Schmeisser MP28: an improved version of the modified MP18/I, conceived by Hugo Schmeisser and made by Haenel, principally for export.

Fire selector of an MP28/II. The lever is here at the position of single shot fire (the letter "E" for *Einzelfeuer* is visible).

Continuing with his work of modernization of the MP/II, Hugo Schmeisser developed a fire mode selector actioned by a lever housed forward of the rear brace of the trigger guard.

This patent was also purchased by Haenel, who applied it to a submachine gun very close to the modified MP18/I, which took the name MP28/II. Like the modified MP18/I, the MP28/II bore "System Schmeisser" in large letters on the magazine housing.

The meaning of "/II," like that of the "/I" in MP18/I, has not been clearly ascertained.

Apart from the presence of a fire mode selector, the MP28/II has several interesting modernizations:

- a large diameter recoil spring much less likely to twist during operation than the smaller diameter one on the MP18/I,

- a solid barrel forward of the receiver, which can be disassembled without having to remove the sight as on the MP18/I,

- a carbine type sight, calibrated from 100 to 1,000 meters, allowing it to be used for long distances.

In order to satisfy the needs of potential buyers, the weapon was proposed in various hand gun calibers in use at the time: 9 mm and 7.65 mm Parabellum, 7.63 mm Mauser, 9 mm Bergmann Bayard. Some prototypes in .45 ACP were also created but seemingly were never mass-produced.

The ease of conversion from one caliber to another is confirmed by a report from the test commission of Versailles dated May 16, 1933 (note No.338A question No.439),this commission which ensured the "old method" to the benefit of the French Army, dealt with an MP28/II which is christened here "MP Schmeisser," having three barrels in 9 mm Parabellum, 7.65 mm Parabellum and 7.63 Mauser, as well as three magazines (one per caliber), two spare foresights marked "7.65" and "7.63," a device to load the magazines and a screwdriver combined. Here is an extract from the report: "After examining the weapon and taking note of the similarities with the PM Bergmann (i.e. the MP18/I), the commission observed the good operation of the weapon in each of the three calibers and the ease of passage from one caliber to the other by changing the barrel and the foresight. It is observed that the 9 mm and 7.65 mm magazines are interchangeable and that the 7.36 mm Mauser only differs from the others by the absence of a rib on its rear side, which enables longer cartridges to be housed. It is noted however that the use of this magazine with 9 mm and 7.65 mm Parabellum cartridges leads to a faultless operation of the PM."

The weapon was exported throughout the world and was even acquired by the French Army. These PMs, bought before the war in Belgium, were probably only used in France in a restricted number.

The manufacture of the MP28/II ended at the end of the thirties. In 1939, the *Wehrmacht* requisitioned the weapons still available at the Haenel factory or in police service.

The weapons were used copiously by the *Wehrmacht* before being transferred to police units when the MP40 started to be available in sufficient number for the needs of the armed forces.

The *Kriegsmarine*, which was supplied with fewer modern infantry weapons, kept the MP28/II until the end of the Second World War.

Some MP28/II used by the police are fitted with a "safety block," whereas others have an MP40 cocking handle, replacing the original hook-shaped bolt handle.

Guard with an MP28/I surveying the gangway of a German U-boat. *ECPA*

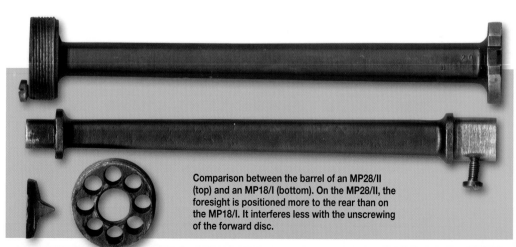

Comparison between the barrel of an MP28/II (top) and an MP18/I (bottom). On the MP28/II, the foresight is positioned more to the rear than on the MP18/I. It interferes less with the unscrewing of the forward disc.

MP 28/II where the original hook shaped bolt handle has been replaced by an MP40 type. The weapon bears the German commercial proof stamp adopted after 1939 (Eagle/N) which bears witness to a curiously late manufacture for this model which was already old at the time.

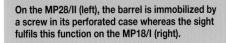

On the MP28/II (left), the barrel is immobilized by a screw in its perforated case whereas the sight fulfils this function on the MP18/I (right).

During the Second World War, the SS and police divisions were frequently armed with the MP28/II. This photo shows a man of the SD, armed with an MP28/II, controlling the inhabitants of Warsaw.

It should be noted that, even though the modified MP18/I magazines could be housed without problem in the MP28/II magazine housing, a difference of a few tenths of a millimeter could prevent the use of MP28/II magazines on modified MP18/I.

Derivatives of the MP28/II

Belgium: The 1934 Model Submachine Gun (MI 34)
When the Belgian army decided to adopt the Schmeisser MP28/II, the exportation of weapons of war from Germany was still subject to restrictions ensuing from the treaty of Versailles. An agreement was made between Haenel and the former Pieper establishments of Liege so that Haenel could deliver unfinished weapons and also weapons devoid of barrels to them, (the export of unfinished weapons seemed to bend the rules) and that the AEP ensured the final finish, the bronzing of the weapons, as well as the assembly of the barrel and their manufacture. This information is confirmed by Michael Druart in his history of the old Pieper establishment in which he mentions a report from the monthly session of the testing stand of the Weapons Manufacturers Union of Liege, dated November 17, 1933, which states: "The former Pieper establishments buy (Schmeisser) submachine guns from abroad and finalize them by making the barrels only."

The agreement initially made between Haenel and Pieper concerned 1,500 weapons with a possible extension to 3,500.

Several Belgian collectors have noted the existence of slight variations in secondary parts (dimensions of the screws, bolt handle, etc.). It is likely that these differences result from attempts at improvement of the German weapon made by Pieper engineers.

The model 34 differed only in terms of its markings from the German version.

Without the origin of this distinctive feature being known, some examples are equipped with a sling ring under the butt and not a base to mount a G.98 sling, as on the MP28/II.

The model 1934 was only used as equipment in a limited number (1,500) for the Belgian army and Gendarmerie and several (probably around thirteen) for the Gendarmerie of the Grand Duchy of Luxembourg.

It has today become highly prized for collectors of submachine guns.

After the invasion of Belgium by German troops, the Pieper PM taken from Belgian troops or seized from Pieper establishments were put back into service in the ranks of the *Wehrmacht* under the name "MP740 (b)."

Before the Second World War, the French army had also placed an order with Pieper for 1,000 Schmeisser submachine guns. The use of the Schmeisser by the French army constitutes a little known fact for amateur students of contemporary military history and indeed the existence of French military instruction notices relative to this weapon is confirmation of use by French troops.

In his article entitled "Submachine Guns and Steel Helmets" ("*Mitraillettes et Bourguignottes*") published in the *Gazette des Armes* on French Second World War submachine guns, François Vauvillier mentions the testimony given by the weapons engineer Happich, director of manufacture of weapons from 1936 to 1939. This testimony was given before the parliamentary commission in charge of investigating events that had taken place in France and during which Happich confirmed the purchase of 1,000 Schmeisser submachine guns.

Standard marking of an MP28/II. Note the commercial Eagle/N proof stamp which came into effect from 1939 and the serial number of the weapon placed lengthways.

Police commando at rest. An MG34 is on the ground on the right, the man on the left has an MP28/II and the man in the center has an MP34. *Georges Delporte*

Another type of marking.

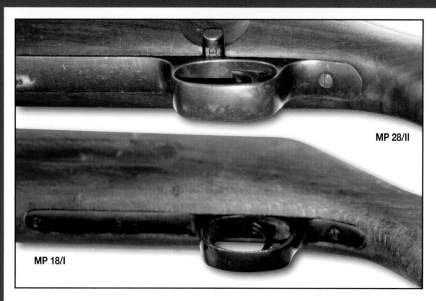

MP 28/II

MP 18/I

Comparison of trigger guards on an MP18/I and MP28/II.

Manufacturer's marking at the front of the magazine housing.

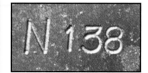

Marking N138 on the magazine housing of an MP28/II. It indicates that this weapon, allocated to the *Kriegsmarine*, belonged to stock of the North Sea naval base arsenal.

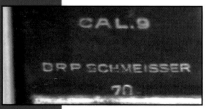

Another type of marking seen on MP28/II magazines: "CAL.9/ DRP Schmeisser/70."

FIA submachine gun fitted with a bolt handle in the form of a large cylindrical button. On this specimen the magazine housing has been painted with a blue-black varnish to make the weapon less visible.

Wehrmacht soldier armed with an MP28/II. *Luc Guillou*

A note in the Technical Establishment of Versailles, conserved in Châtellerault in the weapons archives, summarizes the mission carried out in 1939 by a French officer: Colonel Bacque, who travelled to Belgium to take delivery of the first 300 MP Schmeisser weapons along with 900 magazines, 300 loading tools, 300 multi-purpose tools, 300 rods with two chamber brushes and 60,000 9 mm Parabellum cartridges. It is highly likely that the remainder of this order was never delivered due to the outbreak of the Second World War.

The MP28/IIs made by Haenel and reserved for the German forces and the invasion of Belgium by German troops put an end to the activities of Pieper, which was placed under the administrative supervision of the German company Heinrich Krieghoff and took the name "Heinrich Krieghoff-Werk Lüttich."

Spain

Before the civil war Spain made a copy of the MP28/ II called "subfusil Schmeisser" that the French weapons technical services report designated "FAI submachine gun." These weapons were made in Spain by FAI in Largo 9 mm caliber for the army and in Mauser 7.63 mm caliber for assault troops and the civil guard. This version differs from the German MP28/II by its magazine housing, trigger guard, and its bronze butt plate. The realization of these parts from casts considerably simplified the process of manufacture of the weapon. Some of the submachine guns are equipped with a hook shaped bolt handle, other handles are in the shape of a large ridged button.

The existence of magazines for this weapon, marked "Fabrica de Armas de Cataluna," leads to the supposition that a parallel manufacture was started in Catalonia during the civil war by the republican government.

Other particularities of this Spanish version: the sling rings are circular, the breech cover is ridged and the positions of the fire mode selector are identifiable by the letter "T" for single shot fire (*tiro par tiro*) and "A" for automatic fire (*almethadora*).

During the civil war, Germany sent MP28/II weapons to Spanish nationalists. In 1937, the prohibition of the export of arms from Germany in application of the Treaty of Versailles no longer had an effect as the Weimar Republic, from 1925, had started to free itself from the treaty and the third Reich had totally denounced it.

In the great panic of 1940, the French army, looking to use all submachine guns that it could have at its disposal, turned to the many weapons seized from defeated Spanish republican troops, when they took refuge in France in 1939.

Devices for loading MP28/II magazines with two variations of markings: "System Schmesisser" and "DRP Schmeisser."

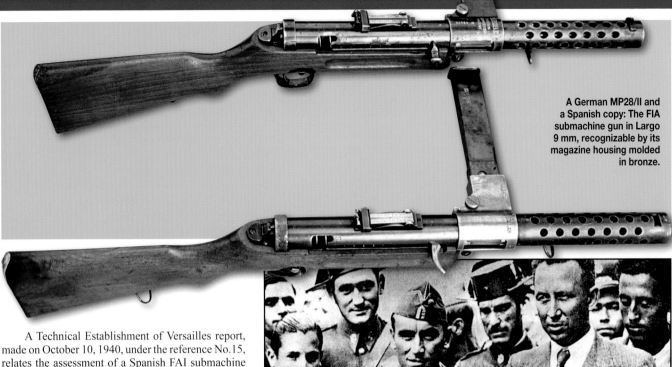

A German MP28/II and a Spanish copy: The FIA submachine gun in Largo 9 mm, recognizable by its magazine housing molded in bronze.

A Technical Establishment of Versailles report, made on October 10, 1940, under the reference No.15, relates the assessment of a Spanish FAI submachine gun (copy of the MP28/II).

This weapon is chambered for Largo 9 mm cartridges which also came from equipment captured at the French-Spanish border and at the time were stocked at the Miramas warehouse.

The commission concluded the test of two submachine guns, bearing the numbers 1A and 88A, with the following comment: "The FAI submachine gun operated satisfactorily, with acceptable accuracy. The relatively slow firing rate makes it agreeable to fire. The fact that this weapon fires the Bergmann 33 mm cartridge, different from other similar weapons that were planned for use, could prove an obstacle for resupplies. In addition, as there were only a small number of FAI submachine guns in the stocks at Clermont-Ferrand, it seems their use by the armies, unless for urgent reasons, is not desirable."

During the Civil War, Spanish soldiers and civil guards examine MP28/IIs brought by a German cargo ship.

Great Britain

When Great Britain was threatened with invasion by the German army in 1940, the country ordered large quantities of 1928 model Thompson submachine guns from the USA. But many of these weapons ended up at the bottom of the Atlantic trapped in the holds of cargo ships sunk by German U-boats (some American authors assess the losses at 300,000 Thompsons out of the 500,000 bought by Great Britain from the USA).

In order to be in a position to equip the Home Guard, to whom Winston Churchill had planned to entrust the harassment of German troops in the event of an invasion, the British chose purely and simply to copy the German 28/II, which appeared to be at that time the simplest weapon to produce.

From left to right: smooth butt plate on an MP18/I and ridged on German and Spanish MP28/II.

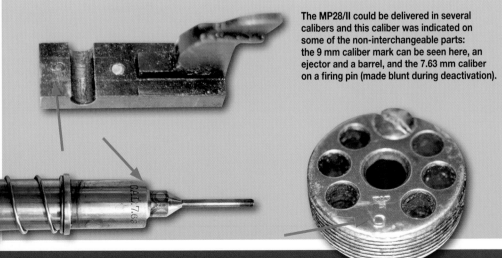

The MP28/II could be delivered in several calibers and this caliber was indicated on some of the non-interchangeable parts: the 9 mm caliber mark can be seen here, an ejector and a barrel, and the 7.63 mm caliber on a firing pin (made blunt during deactivation).

SCHMEISSER

Detail of a "Schmeisser" marking on an MP28/II magazine.

The British Lanchester submachine gun was basically a fairly faithful copy of the German MP28/II and the Sten also bore numerous elements inherited from the "Schmeisser MP."

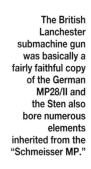

Photo taken from a user manual for the Schmeisser MP28/II, showing a policeman equipped with the weapon and broad "satchel" type magazine pouches.

Characteristics of the MP18/I and the MP28/II		
	MP18/I	MP28/II
Caliber	9 mm Parabellum	9 mm and 7.65 Parabellum, 9 mm Bergamnn Bayard, 7.63 mm Mauser, .45 ACP (experimental)
Total length	815 mm	815 mm
Barrel length	20 cm	20 cm
Empty weight	4.2 kg	4 kg
Loaded weight	5.25 kg	4.7 kg
Selective fire capability	No	Yes
Firing rate	500 shots per minute approx.	500 shots per minute approx.
Sight	Bracket calibrated for distances between 100 and 200 meters	Carbine sight calibrated from 100 to 1,000 meters
Magazine	32-round drum magazine on the initial version. Straight 20-round magazines on the modified version.	10-, 20-, 32-, and 50-round magazines.

From left to right: a smooth MP18/I butt plate and German and Spanish ridged MP28/II butt plate.

FIA magazine made for the republican army by the war industry of Catalonia during the civil war.

20- and 32-round magazines for MP28/II. The 20-round magazines were mainly used by the German police.

The authorities entrusted George Stirling, an engineer of the automobile firm Lanchester, with the task of setting up the manufacture of copies of two MP28/II weapons supplied by the British Consul in Addis Ababa. George Stirling redesigned the parts of the MP28/II to British dimensions and chose to make the magazine housing in cast bronze, as the Spanish had done earlier, in order to simplify the machining process of the weapon. It was also equipped with a butt presenting the same profile as the Lee-Enfield rifle along with a stud necessary to fix the Lee-Enfield Mk.III bayonet. Stirling also equipped his weapon with a fire mode selector positioned at the front of the trigger guard.

Several months later, the arsenal at Enfield proposed a submachine gun that was simpler to manufacture than the one conceived by its two technicians: Reginald V. Shepherd and Harold Turpin. The weapon, christened STEN (made up of the initials of Shepherd, Turpin and Enfield) rapidly replaced the Lanchester whose manufacture was stopped in 1942. With more than four million STENs made, in the end it was a fairly faithful and highly simplified copy of the MP28/II.

Schmeisser patented multi-purpose screwdriver delivered with the MP28/II. This tool had a blade at each end of differing widths to fit different screws and at the center two studs used for the disassembly of the weapon.

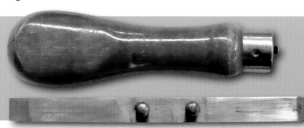

CHAPTER 4

THE BERGMANN MP35/I

MP35/I with a walnut butt. This example, with no markings other than the serial number and proof stamp "N crowned," probably corresponds to the first make of this model, made in Germany by Walther.

The mechanism imagined by Müller bore a breech actioned by a lever positioned at the rear left on the right side, which had four parts to the maneuver, like a Mauser rifle. This lever remained immobile during fire unlike bolt handles on MP18/1 and 28/II. Bergmann patented this system on July 6, 1932.

At that time, the Bergmann workshops at Suhl and Gagneau, which had produced the initial and modified MP18/1 had disappeared, like so many other German enterprises left ruined by the war and the economic crash which followed it. Bergmann started to look for an industrial firm capable of manufacturing its MP in a country bordering Germany, in order to avoid coming under the zone of influence of German firms being forbidden from manufacturing arms imposed by the Treaty of Versailles.

Eventually the German company approached the Danish firm Schultz and Larsen in Otterup to make prototypes of its weapon. The Danish company, reputed for its competition carbines, produced around 2,000 Bergmann submachine guns in 9 mm Parabellum and in two barrel lengths: in 20 cm which was the version christened "BMP 32" (MP Bergmann model 1932) and the 32 cm called BMK 32 (Bergmann automatic carbine model 1932).

A user manual was written, in order to praise the superiority of the Bergmann MP over other weapons of the same type on the market at that time. Some Bergmann prototypes were proposed to various European armies after which they received only polite interest initially.

Left: interesting color photo of a soldier of the *Wehrmacht* with an MP35/I.

German customs "R.F.V." marking (*Reichsfinanzvervwaltung*).

The MP35/I, which was adopted during the Second World War by the *Waffen-SS*, was a consequence of the rather chaotic development of a weapon, which appeared at the beginning of the 1930s when Theodor Emil Bergmann, son of Theodor Bergmann, joined forces with an engineer by the name of Müller to develop a new type of submachine gun conceived to reduce jamming incidents caused by foreign bodies entering the mechanism of the submachine guns.

The technical part of the project was attributed to Müller whereas Bergmann ensured the marketing of the weapon. The former division of roles that had previously existed at the time between Bergmann: the organizer and sales; and Schmeisser, the inventors and technicians.

Presentation

The Bergmann MP has an open bolt with no other exterior part mobile during firing.

The trigger has a system which initiates single shot fire when the user presses it lightly and by continuous burst fire if the trigger is pressed hard.

Comparison between the two markings on an MP35/I at the beginning of the war on which the enterprise Junkers & Ruh still marked its stylized initials and an example made in 1942 by the same company, marked only with the code ajf.

Second type of safety (B) composed of a lever placed on the left side of the receiver. This weapon has another type of safety of the "Blocksicherung" type (A) added by the police and the disassembly lever of the breech can also be seen (C).

Junker & Ruh with a butt in beech.

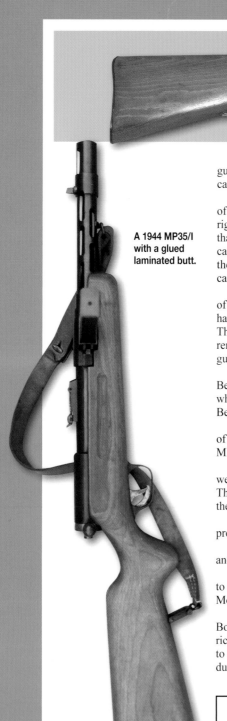

A 1944 MP35/I with a glued laminated butt.

At its extreme rear the barrel has two vertical guides designed to ensure an improved guidance of the cartridges (a device copied on the SIG 1920).

The MP Bergmann presents the curious particularity of being fed by a lateral magazine, positioned on the right side of the weapon. It can therefore be concluded that the designers envisaged it being handled like a carbine, where the handguard is permanently held by the shooter's weak hand, whereas the strong hand carries out loading and operating the trigger.

Logically, a safety catch is positioned at the rear of the mobile breech. The user operates it with the right hand in the same way as the safety on a Mauser carbine. The rear of the receiver has a recoil buffer which is reminiscent of that on the Finnish Suomi submachine gun of the same period.

In 1934, Theodor Bergmann founded the "Theodor Bergmann & Co GmbH" company with Dietrich Stahl, which had the task of marketing, rather than producing, Bergmann weapons.

For this task, he spoke to the Carl Walther Company of Zella-Mehlis who agreed to make the Bergmann MP and produced around 2,000 in 1934 and 1935.

Like the BMP 32, the first MP34 submachine guns were fitted with a recoil buffer at the rear of the breech. This system was rapidly abandoned and the weapon then took the name MP34/I.

As done previously, two barrel lengths were proposed for this model (20 or 32 cm).

The MP34/I was adopted by Denmark, Bolivia, and Ethiopia.

In 1935, the MP34/I had its safety repositioned to the rear of the breech to the left side of the receiver. Modified in this way, it took the name of MP35/I.

Some MP34/I and 35/I weapons were sold to Bolivia while at war with Paraguay for control of the rich mining region of Chaco. Other weapons were sold to Ethiopia and would be used by the troops of Negus during the Italian invasion.

The very thin grip on the butt was a weak point on the MP35/I, as the slits visible on these two examples show.

Close up of the early markings on the Junker & Ruh, also visible is the SS Zeugmat 1 stamp.

Close up of a 1942 made weapon; the last marking is an SS *Zeugmat* stamp.

Gebirgsjäger armed with an MP35/I.

In 1939, Sweden also adopted the Bergmann under the name "Kulsprutpistol m/39" (Kpist m/39) and ordered 1,800 in both barrel lengths.

Apart from these official markets, other Bergmanns were fraudulently exported to Spain, where the Nazi regime, recently in power, gave its support to the pro-Franco rebellion.

The SS Enters the Scene

Despite these various orders, official or otherwise, the "Theodor Bergmann & Co GmbH" company experienced financial difficulties which led Bergmann to withdraw from its association with Dietrich Stahl.

Around 1938, Dietrich Stahl was approached by an SS emissary who offered to take all unsold, Walther-made submachine guns and asked him to organize a new manufacture of 45,000 weapons.

The SS organization was in fact in the process of developing a military branch, which was to result in the *Waffen-SS*, but the *Wehrmacht* did not allow it to benefit from deliveries from established German companies.

Stahl made an agreement with a firm specializing in the manufacture of cookers and car supplies: Junker & Ruh, which agreed to make MP35/I and thus to help out the redoubtable SS.

The first deliveries to the *Waffen-SS* were made in 1940 and continued gradually throughout the war. This version of the MP35 with a 20 cm barrel took the name of the MP35/I. The first examples were marked with "JR," the initials of the manufacturer which, from 1940, were to be replaced by the code "ajf" attributed to Junker & Ruh by the *Waffenamt*.

These two MP35/I weapons, one with a butt in walnut and the other glued and laminated, seen here with a 24 model stick grenade and other objects evoking the close association of this weapon with Nazi security forces. *Collection of the Royal Army Museum of Brussels, photo by Marc de Fromont*

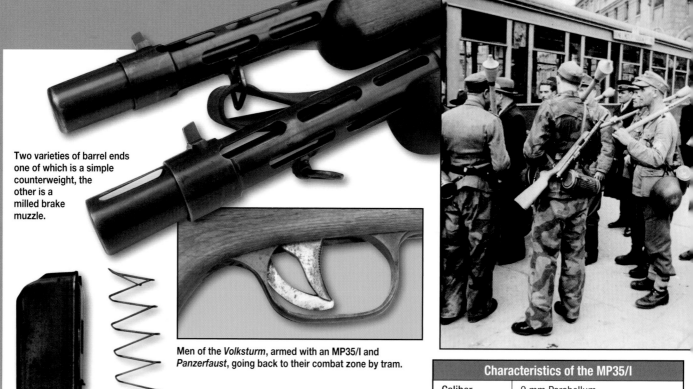

Two varieties of barrel ends one of which is a simple counterweight, the other is a milled brake muzzle.

Men of the *Volksturm*, armed with an MP35/I and *Panzerfaust*, going back to their combat zone by tram.

An MP35/I disassembled 20-round magazine. Note that the base has a latch limiting the depression of the magazine follower.

Subsequently Junker & Ruh were to deliver the MP35/I to various police organizations, regrouped from 1936 under the authority of the *Reichsführer-SS* Heinrich Himmler, as well as the German customs. The weapons destined for the customs were marked with the initials "RFV" (*Reichsfinanzverwaltung*) at the rear of the breech, but they bear the SS *Zeugmat* No.1 stamp, the organization responsible for checking that the quality of equipment delivered to the "Black Order" was equivalent to those of the *Waffenamt* and *Wehrmacht*.

The ordered placed with Junker & Ruh would never be completely finalized: at the end of November 1943 only 1,800 MP35/I s had been delivered out of 4,500 ordered. The weapons ministry therefore gave the order to halt manufacture of these submachine guns entirely made of machined parts and using a high amount of both raw materials and qualified labor.

Characteristics of the MP35/I	
Caliber	9 mm Parabellum
Total length	840 mm
Barrel length	200 mm
Weight	4.1 kg (empty), 4.7 kg (loaded)
Rate of fire	600 to 650 shots per minute
Ammunition	20- and 32-round magazines

The first MP43 weapons, made rapidly and in large quantities from parts made of pressed sheet metal, started coming off the production lines at that time. However, the manufacture of 7.92 Kurz cartridges destined for the MP43 did not keep up with the increase in need. Thus the weapons ministry authorized Junkers & Ruh to temporarily take up the manufacture of the MP35/I until 1944, the date when production was definitively stopped (like other submachine guns made in Germany up until that time) in favor of the MP43.

MP 35/I rudimentarily disassembled.

Left: breech with notch for the *"Blocksicherung"* (arrow).
Right: non-modified breech.

CHAPTER 5

THE MP34(ö) STEYR SOLOTHURN

Steyr Solothurn Mauser 9 mm caliber submachine gun requisitioned by the *Wehrmacht* and put into service under the name MP34 (ö).

Early production Steyr Solothurn SI-100 submachine gun, identifiable by the particular shape of the butt.

Founded in 1888, the Rheinmetall ammunition factory had bought the old Dreyse factory in 1901, and continued its rise until the First World War, when it became one of the main suppliers of artillery pieces and ammunition of the German army.

Closely linked to the Krupp company, during the war Rheinmetall also manufactured small caliber weapons, in particular for Maxim MG 08 machine guns.

Rheinmetall was greatly affected by the defeat in 1918, and was prevented from continuing its activities in research and manufacture of weapons by the Allies. The company, fifty-one percent of which was in reality owned by the German government, secretly transferred 23,000 tons of equipment and documents to the Netherlands from where its employees could continue with their research.

Sales, the presentation of the products along with the testing of finished weapons was assured by the Dutch subsidiary whereas the weapons were in fact made in Austria by Steyr-Daimler Puch AG.

16 Stck. 9 mm Mauser-Pistolenpatronen
P 635, 11. L. 40
Nz. Stb. P. n./A. (0,8·0,6) : Rottw. 1. L. 38
Patrh.: P 635. 14. L. 40. Gesch.: P 635. 3. L. 40
Zdh.: G. 10. L. 40

Box of sixteen 9 mm Mauser cartridges on two eight clips, designed for the MP34 chambered for this caliber.

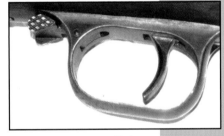

Safety positioned in front of the trigger guard on an early version of the SI-100.

Meanwhile in Switzerland, a former director of the DWM company, Hans von Steiger, had bought a failing watchmaking factory for a low price. This enterprise in Solothurn was liquidated in 1923 to be converted into a weapons and ammunitions factory. In 1928, von Steiger gave up his business to an Austrian named Mandl. In an in-depth study of the Solothurn firm (*Swiss Connection*, 2007) German historian Michael Heidler believes that Fritz Mandl was acting behind the scenes for the Austrian ammunitions company Hirtenberger, with the intention of eliminating a competitor.

In April 1929, Mandl gave ninety percent of his company shares to Rheinmetall and kept his job as director of the Solothurn factory.

At the same time the German government also took control of the Austrian company Steyr-Daimler Puch AG by the intermediary of Rheinmetall.

From then on, Solothurn took care of the final assembly of the parts for submachine guns and light machine guns made in Germany and Austria then discreetly exported to Switzerland. The weapons assembled by Solothurn had the appearance of having been made in a neutral country that had no restrictions in terms of raw materials or sales, in that way therefore they could be exported throughout the whole world for the benefit of Rheinmetall and Steyr-Daimler Puch AG.

Steyr trade mark on an MP34 (ö) of the *Luftwaffe*.

Magazine pouch delivered to Portugal. Photos of the period show that the German army and police used similar ones between 1939 and 1945.

The SI-100 was the object of small contracts for central European countries, Asia and Latin America: here is a Japanese soldier with a Steyr Solothurn submachine gun.

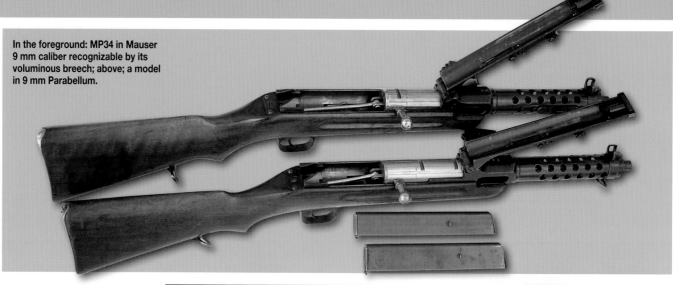

In the foreground: MP34 in Mauser 9 mm caliber recognizable by its voluminous breech; above; a model in 9 mm Parabellum.

Steyr-Solothurn submachine guns have the particularity of being equipped with a magazine clip guide on the upper part of the magazine housing and having a bolt on its lower part allowing the magazine to be held in a vertical position while the user loads the weapon with 8-round magazine clips of the same type used on the Steyr 1912 model pistol.

Marking on the butt of the Portuguese contract Steyr-Solothurn.

Military marking: code 660 on a 1939 dated *Luftwaffe* gun.

Reception stamp of the *Luftwaffe* on the butt of an MP34 (ö) in Mauser 9 mm. The *Wehrmacht* preferred to supply weapons which were not chambered for the regulation 9 mm Parabellum to units that were not directly engaged in front-line combat: police, protection of air bases etc.

Another type of magazine pouch used with the Steyr-Solothurn. This is most likely material made in Anschluss for the Austrian police and gendarmerie. These were also used by the *Wehrmacht* and the German police during the Second World War.

Presentation

The designers of the Steyr Solothurn wanted to realize a short and compact weapon which was also stable and accurate during continuous burst fire.

The main solution proposed to answer these demands consisted in positioning the recoil spring in the butt and to transmit the breech movements by means of an articulated rod. This system meant the length of the receiver was reduced, the center of gravity of the weapon was slightly repositioned towards the rear compared with the MP18/I and 28/II, and the movements of the weapon during both single shot and continuous burst fire were diminished.

The relatively increased weight of this weapon reinforced its stability and in addition the excellent quality of the materials along with the careful machining of standard parts on the Steyr made it an especially accurate and robust weapon, stable during firing.

The Steyr Solothurn constituted therefore at that time a remarkable combat tool offering its users an impressive firepower while keeping its highly satisfactory accuracy.

The fire mode selector is operated by a lever moving horizontally from the left side of the handguard, which a right-handed shooter could easily operate with the thumb of the left hand. Pushed to the rear (position "E" on weapons destined for German speaking countries), it allowed single shot fire (*Einzelfeuer*). Pushed to the front (position "D") it permitted continuous burst fire (*Dauerfeuer*).

The gunsights were composed of a backsight with leaf and slide and a triangular foresight mounted on a dovetail and protected by two robust lateral braces. The sighting notch and the foresight are of ample dimensions so as to remain visible in dim light.

The barrel, protected by a tubular jacket with cooling slots, is disassembled by simply unscrewing with a hexagonal key, kept in the maintenance kit supplied with each weapon.

On the majority of models the magazine housing, slightly inclined to the front, is equipped with a guide and an unscrewing system, which allows the magazines to be blocked in a vertical position to load them with 8-round loading clips.

Young *Luftwaffe* soldier carrying both a K.98k, and an MP34(ö). *ECPA*

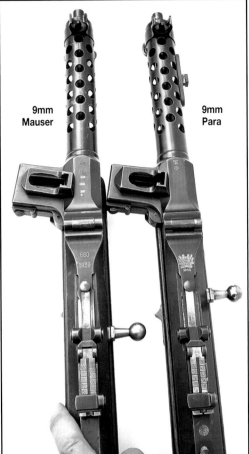

9mm Mauser   9mm Para

Steyr Solothurn transport cover adopted by the Portuguese army.

In 1943, Steyr Daimler Puch delivered several hundred Steyr Solothurns to the Portuguese army (right, on the photo). These weapons, chambered in 9 mm Parabellum, were christened m/943. They were resold on the French market after being deactivated around 1990 and were the most common version of the Steyr Solothurn.

Sight calibrated up to 500 m, safety catch (A), and cover release catch of the MP34(ö) (B).

The magazines contained thirty-two cartridges in double stack double feed ensuring the cartridges were presented alternately on the left lip then on the right.

The receiver is covered by a hinged lid, bolted at the rear, which gives easy access to the breech and its push rod.

The butt plate has a hinged flap which gives easy access to the head of the buffer pitot of the recoil spring in order to disassemble the weapon.

Variations and Use

Having begun manufacture in 1934, the production was halted on the Steyr-Solothurn submachine gun in 1940 in favor of the MP40.

A final delivery was made in Portugal late 1942/early 1943, but it is likely that these weapons were not the object of a new manufacturing cycle but were assembled from spare parts still available at the factory.

Adopted by the Austrian police in Steyr (9x23 mm) 9 mm caliber and by the Austrian army in Mauser 9 mm caliber, the Steyr Solothurn was subject to small exportation contracts to different countries including: Bolivia, which used them against Paraguay in the Chaco War, Greece, and probably Bulgaria.

When Austria was annexed by Germany in 1937, the *Wehrmacht* requisitioned the production of Austrian weapons factories.

The Steyr-Solothurn submachine gun was integrated in the list of German regulation weapons under the name MP34(ö). The majority of examples available were given to units of the *Luftwaffe* and the police. A

Characteristics of the MP34(ö)	
Caliber	9mm Mauser or 9 mm Steyr (9 mm Parabellum for the Portuguese version m/943 and some other versions for export)
Total length	81 cm
Barrel length	20 cm
Empty weight	4.3 kg
Loaded weight	4.9 kg
Magazine capacity	32 cartridges (4 magazine clips of 8)
Firing Rate	Around 700 shots per minute

report from the ETVS (Technical Establishment of Versailles) recounting the examination of an MP34(ö) captured in combat during the "phony war" indicated that the German infantry also used some of these weapons in the period 1939–40. The majority of them were chambered for ammunition other than the regulation 9 mm Parabellum, the *Wehrmacht* was keen however to donate them to the *Luftwaffe* and the police, as soon as they had enough MP40 in sufficient number for their own needs.

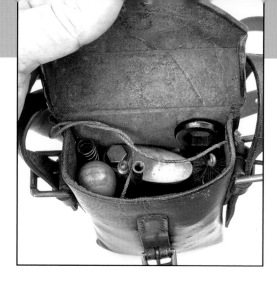

Maintenance kit delivered with every Portuguese contract submachine gun.

Before taking the road, the driver checks his MP34(ö).

Croatian marking added on the receiver of the weapon by the Ustacha.

In 1942, the Third Reich received an order from Portugal for P.08 pistols, Steyr-Solothurn submachine guns, and MG 34 and 42. The Reich, then at the height of its powers, agreed to supply these weapons to this country which had proved to be of a benevolent neutrality and which could, because of the resources in its African colonies, contribute to the supply of various raw materials to German industry that were not available in the territories of occupied Europe.

The Steyr Solothurn of the Portuguese contract are chambered in 9 mm Parabellum, a caliber that Portugal had decided to adopt consistently for its handguns and its submachine guns in place of the 7.65 mm Parabellum used from the beginning of the twentieth century. Portugal Arms, along with the year 1942, were stamped on the top of the chamber and the butt. The positions of the fire mode selector are referenced by the letter "T" for single shot fire and "S" for continuous burst fire instead of "E" and "D" on the German models.

The rarest version of the submachine gun was without doubt this Steyr Solothurn with commercial markings, bearing a Greek hallmark on the butt; the letter indicators for the fire mode selector are in the Greek alphabet and the receiver bears the Croatian coat of arms above the letter "U," which denotes the use of the weapon by the Ustacha. This Nationalist Croatian movement led by Dr. Ante Palvelich was a faithful ally of the Reich during the Second World War and it is not surprising that the *Wehrmacht* was able to transfer weapons captured in 1940 to the Greek army to support the Oustachis in their fight against the communist supporters of Tito.

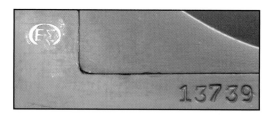

Markings on a Steyr Solothurn delivered before 1939 to the Greek security police then captured by the Germans in 1940, and transferred to the Ustacha Croat nationalists.

Disassembled Steyr Solothurn MP34(ö).

CHAPTER 6

THE "EMP" (ERMA VOLLMER) SUBMACHINE GUN

Vollmer submachine gun without protective jacket, made in 1933 and christened VPH: the meaning of which remains unknown. *Photo by Michael Heidler*

This very promising submachine gun came into being around 1920 from the imagination of a German metallurgist: Heinrich Vollmer.

The young Heinrich had already made his mark in 1909 when, at age twenty-four, he conceived a bullet-proof vest that he proposed to the Prussian war ministry without much success.

Deeply patriotic, he signed up to the German army from the beginning of the First World War, but his superiors managed to convince him that during this period the country had as much need of metallurgists and engineers as it did soldiers.

Heinrich Vollmer consequently returned to civilian life to manufacture muzzle covers that the army needed for its Mausers.

During the war, he founded a company specializing in the manufacture of aviation propeller blades (airplanes and Zeppelin) the "Erstes Süddeutsches Propellerwerke." The assistance he brought to the German aviation industry saw him awarded with the Cross of Merit of Württemberg.

Man in a police unit armed with an EMP.

The marking of the EMP was reduced to the strict minimum: EMP and the serial number also appear on the magazine housing and breech.

Marking on the weapon.
Photo by Michael Heidler

In parallel with this activity, Heinrich Vollmer maintained a strong interest in weapons; he developed several ammunition systems for machine guns which did not use ammo belts, often the cause of feeding incidents.

The German army was extremely interested in this Vollmer ammunition system for its heavy T.u.F. 13 mm caliber which was under development, but the end of the war brought an end to this project.

Heinrich Vollmer, who had known the efficiency of the first MP18/I submachine guns used by German assault troops during the offensive of 1918, had a great interest in this type of weapon. It is likely he developed prototypes under cover of secrecy and with the support of the *Reichswehr.* Various Vollmer prototypes were tried out by the German army between 1925 and 1928 at the same time as the Bergmann and Rheinmetall submachine gun prototypes, some with a barrel protected by a perforated jacket others with a non-protected barrel.

Vollmer's initial prototype was equipped with a 25-round drum magazine which seemingly caused operational problems and had been quite difficult to load. Vollmer therefore abandoned this magazine as the capacity was insufficient in relation to the specifications of the *Reichswehr.*

In 1928, Vollmer presented a new prototype called VMPi (*Vollmer Maschinenpistole*), fitted with a 35-round box magazine positioned horizontally on the left side of the weapon. Later the breech system was rethought and reconfigured to ensure a simplified disassembly and resulted in the famous Vollmer breech where the recoil spring is contained in a telescopic metal tube.

Three-fold increase in sighting. *Photo by Michael Heidler*

Markings on the barrel on a VMPi: this weapon bears the serial number 6 and is chambered in Mauser 7.63 mm. *Photo by Michael Heidler*

Disassembled 1933 VPH: the breech is still fitted with an independent recoil spring. *Photo by Michael Heidler*

Standard EMP. This example is equipped with a 20-round cartridge magazine and fitted with a safety block ("*Blocksicherung*"), regulation in the police.

EMP in service in the police, equipped with a *Blocksicherung* and marked with a police reception stamp: "Eagle K."

Receiver of an EMP with disassembled safety block: a groove can be seen in the receiver and the mobile breech where the safety part is housed, to prevent accidental return of the breech.

Early made Vollmer submachine gun (VMPi) fitted with a grooved barrel that can be dismantled.

The telescopic breech patented by Vollmer had a recoil spring protected by a sliding tube inside the breech which simultaneously prevents foreign bodies from getting between the spirals of the spring and stops them from twisting during firing. In addition, this arrangement considerably facilitated the disassembly of the weapon.

The manufacture of prototypes for tests by the Reichswehr and of several hundred weapons from Bulgaria was not enough to guarantee the prosperity of the Vollmer enterprise.

To avoid bankruptcy, Heinrich Vollmer sold his patents to Bertold Geipel, the owner of the ERMA company (abbreviation of Erfurter Maschinenfabrik), with whom he was already in contact as it had been outsourced by VPMi to make some components.

After having abandoned the manufacture of its submachine gun, Heinrich Vollmer continued with weapons research and developed the 35 model automatic carbine (MKb 35), firing an intermediary cartridge, which heralded the 7.92 kurz which would be adopted at the end of the war by the *Wehrmacht* for its MP43 assault rifle.

Taking advantage of the relaxation in the application of the Treaty of Versailles, Giepel took out a patent to cover the promising mechanism of the Vollmer breech (DRP No.580,620 of July 13, 1933) and openly launched mass production of the Vollmer submachine gun under the name "EMP" (*Erma Maschinenpistole*).

Presentation

The EMP is a submachine gun with a non-fixed breech, with open firing. It is fed by a lateral magazine positioned on the left side. Both 20- and 32-round magazines were proposed to users.

The weapon is fitted with a wooden butt with half pistol grip which stops half way up the weapon and bears a vertical grip.

A fire mode selector is positioned above the trigger guard on the right side.

Depending on the version, the sight could be either tangential and calibrated up to 1,000 meters or a notched flip over leaf rear sight calibrated for 100 and 200 meters.

The principal originality of the EMP resides in its recoil spring housed in a cylindrical tube sliding in the breech. This concept would be taken up by the 38 model Beretta and above all the MP38 and MP40. It presents two advantages:

EMP fitted with a telescopic rest housed in the forward grip. Only a very small number of this version was made.

EMP with a long barrel with bayonet holder sold to Yugoslavia.
Thomas B. Nelson

1. protects the recoil spring from foreign bodies;

2. greatly facilitates the disassembly and assembly of the weapon whereas the presence of a free recoil spring renders this difficult in the field.

Very stable during firing and relatively accurate, the EMP was to be considered as the weapon of reference during tests led by the majority of armies with the objective of adopting a submachine gun between the wars.

Variations and Use

The EMP was initially proposed in three versions:

- with or without a pierced barrel nut.

- equipped with a telescopic mono-pode housed in the forward grip.

- with the pierced barrel nut, equipped with a bayonet stud. In the first volume of his work *The World's Submachine Guns*, Thomas B. Nelson mentions that this version was acquired by the Kingdom of Yugoslavia.

- with a butt fitted with a pistol grip at the front or with a simple butt with no grip (in the style of MP28/II).

- with a tangential sight or with an "L" shaped butt.

The EMP submachine gun was mainly used by the police forces of the Third Reich. *Collection of the Royal Army Museum of Brussels, photo by Marc de Fromont*

Comparison between sling fixations: German on the left and Spanish on the right.

Bulgarian militia: on the left an EMP with a barrel with no perforated case (unless it is a VMPi), on the right a Steyr Solothurn.

D and E stamped on the frame to indicate single shot and continuous burst firing positions on a German EMP.

This safety lever positioned under the handguard, typical of the Spanish made EMP (MP41/44), played the same role as the "*Blocksicherung*" on the German EMP.

Safety block mounted on three police submachine guns: at the back a modified MP18/I, center an MP35/I, and at the front an EMP.

Around 1932, the production seemed to stabilize around a standard model, fitted with a 23 cm barrel, with a notched flip over leaf rear sight for distances between 100 and 200 meters and a pass-through for a sling across the butt as is found on Mauser K98k carbines.

This version was bought around 1933 by the SS, which equipped its detachments with the skull (*Totenkopfverbande*), armed groups of the SS prefiguring the future *Waffen-SS*.

Even though it was not adopted officially, the EMP was also bought by the *Wehrmacht* which, while waiting for the future MP38 to be delivered in sufficient quantities, equipped its troops up until the middle of the war. At that time, as the MP38 and 40 were available in sufficient quantity, the *Wehrmacht* replaced its EMPs with the MP40 and transferred the ERMA to units of the *Waffen-SS* and the police where they were used up to the end of the war.

The German police fitted the weapons in its possession with a "safety block" and had them stamped with the reception stamp: a stylized eagle with a letter "L."

On the international market, the EMP was commercialized in 9 mm and 7.65 mm Parabellum, also in 7.63 mm Mauser and probably in 9 mm Bergmann Bayard.

Before the Second World War, ERMA exported many submachine guns to Bolivia, which was engaged in the Chaco War, as well as Spain where the civil war had created huge needs in submachine guns and also to the new republics of central Europe: Poland and Yugoslavia.

It seems that the manufacture of the EMP stopped at ERMA after the MP38 entered into service. On the eve of the declaration of war in 1939, ERMA proposed its submachine gun to the French army by the intermediary of a Swiss dummy company. This proposition was without consequence.

When the defeated Republican fighters took refuge in France in 1938, they had to leave their weapons at the border. Among them, almost 3,000 EMPs, that would be stored in the regional equipment reserve at Clermont-Ferrand before being redistributed to the *Corps Francs* in 1939.

The origin of the EMP, used during the civil war and later retrieved by the French army, is more complex.

Characteristics of the EMP	
Caliber	9 mm Parabellum
Total length	89 cm (up to 95 cm for long barreled versions)
Barrel length	25 cm
Firing rate	Around 500 shots/minute
Empty weight	4.1 kg
Full weight	4.7 kg
Magazine capacity	20 or 32 cartridges

It is difficult to say today if it concerned German-made weapons exported to Spain or copies of EMP made in Spain. The fact that the weapons bore no markings, apart from several with a serial number, and that deactivation prevented the ascertainment of their caliber rendered the answer very difficult. However, the test reports carried out by the technical departments of the French army, before the submachine guns were put back into service in the armies, mentions that they were chambered in 9 mm Parabellum, except for some which used the Mauser 7.63 mm cartridge. (ETVS report of May 31, 1940, question 570). The chambering in 9 mm Parabellum possibly means that it concerned weapons manufactured in Germany and delivered to Spain before or during the civil war. In this regard, Albert Merglen, member of a *Corps Francs* operating in the Ardennes in 1940, brings his precious testimony in his work *Groupe Franc* (published by Arthaud 1943): "Even the old dream of Corps Francs was coming true: there are German submachine guns that must have come from Spain, and boxes of 9 mm ammunition bearing German inscriptions, date of manufacture 1917. Excellent weapons, easy to handle, light, with the speed of fire necessary in action which cannot of course replace the carbine at 400 meters, but are indispensable in this virtually hand to hand combat through the woods."

Only the lack of magazines assuaged this enthusiasm as the retrieved ERMA only had, at best, one spare magazine per weapon.

Several years later, the Franco regime started making a national version of the EMP destined for its army and forces of order. This Spanish version, called MP41/44, was chambered in the regulation Spanish 9 mm caliber of "9 mm Largo" (9x23 mm). This version is equipped with a breech locking knob placed under the handguard.

In order to allow collectors to distinguish the German versions of the MP41/44 from the Spanish ones, much more available on the market, we have published several photos in this chapter comparing the two weapons.

A short version without barrel nut, called VPK, was also produced in a small quantity after the Second World War in Spain.

Ready to Write a Book?

Our authors are as passionate as we are about providing new and intriguing perspectives on a variety of topics, both niche and general. If you have a fresh idea, we would love to hear from you, as we are continually seeking new authors and their work. Visit our website to view our complete list of titles and our current catalogs. Please visit our Author Resource Center on our website for submission guidelines, and contact us at proposals@schifferbooks.com or write to the address below, to the attention of Acquisitions.

◎ Schiffer Publishing Ltd.

A family-owned, independent publisher since 1974, Schiffer has published thousands of titles on the diverse subjects that fuel our readers' passions. Explore our list of more than 5,000 titles in the following categories:

ART, DESIGN & ANTIQUES
Fine Art | Fashion | Architecture | Interior Design | Landscape | Decorative Arts | Pop Culture | Collectibles | Art History | Graffiti & Street Art | Photography | Pinup | |Sculpture | Body Art & Tattoo | Antique Clocks | Watches | Graphic Design | Contemporary Craft | Illustration | Folk Art | Jewelry | Fabric Reference

MILITARY
Aviation | Naval | Ground Forces | American Civil War | Militaria | Modeling & Collectible Figures | Pinup | Transportation | World War I & II | Uniforms & Clothing | Biographies & Memoirs | Unit Histories | Emblems & Patches | Weapons & Artillery

CRAFT
Arts & Crafts | Fiber Arts & Wearables | Woodworking | Quilts | Gourding | Craft Techniques | Leathercraft | Carving | Boat Building | Knife Making | Printmaking | Weaving | How-to Projects | Tools | Calligraphy

TRADE
Lifestyle | Natural Sciences | History | Children's | Regional | Cookbooks | Entertaining | Guide Books | Wildlife | Tourism | Pets | Puzzles & Games | Movies | Business & Legal | Paranormal | UFOs | Cryptozoology | Vampires | Ghosts

MIND BODY SPIRIT
Divination | Meditation | Astrology | Numerology & Palmistry | Psychic Skills | Channeled Material | Metaphysics | Spirituality | Health & Lifestyle | Tarot & Oracles | Crystals | Wicca | Paganism | Self Improvement

MARITIME
Professional Maritime Instruction \ Seamanship \ Navigation | First Aid/Emergency | Maritime History | The Chesapeake | Antiques & Collectibles | Children's | Crafts | Natural Sciences | Hunting & Fishing | Cooking | Shipping | Sailing | Travel | Navigation

SCHIFFER PUBLISHING, LTD.
4880 Lower Valley Road | Atglen, PA 19310
Phone: 610-593-1777
E-mail: Info@schifferbooks.com
Printed in China

www.schifferbooks.com

CHAPTER 7

THE MP38

With its telescopic breech the EMP brought a notable progress compared with other submachine guns in service.

In January 1938, while the new *Wehrmacht* was planning the increase in power of its armored and parachutist units, the *Waffenamt* placed an order with ERMA for a folding butt version of its EPM, in order to supply its assault troops with a compact weapon with a considerable firepower.

ERMA came up with a prototype derived from the EMP which had been developed several years earlier: the EMP 36, a weapon fitted with a folding butt and a clear barrel bearing a part in the shape of a hinged hook under the muzzle, designed to prevent the accidental recoil of the barrel inside a vehicle, or from a fortification when the weapon was used through a porthole or a loophole.

This light and stylish weapon is made by a traditional machining method and has a fire mode selector as well as fittings in walnut.

The EMP 36. It was from this prototype, realized in secret by the ERMA at the time when Germany was rearming, that the MP36 was able to be developed very rapidly. Produced in a very small quantity, the EMP 36 is today an extremely rare weapon as only two are known to exist: bearing the serial number 1 and 14. The first is in the military museum in Prague while the second, which belonged to *Reichsmarschall* Hermann Göring, was seized by American troops from his residence in Karinhall. This weapon is now in a private American collection. *Photo by Michael Heidler*

Marking of the sub-contractor on the grip.

Code 122 on an MP38 made by Haenel in 1940.

ERMA did not delay in extrapolating a simplified and improved version adapted to mass production. The new ERMA submachine gun was fitted with a grip in cast aluminum, covered in fixings in bakelite and had no fire mode selector, just as the incline of the magazine towards the front had been abandoned on the MP36, which was supposed to improve the control of the weapon during automatic fire.

This submachine gun, developed in a record time of five months, was adopted by the *Wehrmacht* on June 29, 1938, under the name MP38.

Bearing in mind the international tension engendered by the crisis in the Sudetenland and the risk of war with France and Great Britain, it was ordered that this model be manufactured immediately. ERMA was able to begin mass production from July 1938, this short period of time is perhaps illustrative of the fact the manufacture had been anticipated for several months.

In the month of August 1938, the *Wehrmacht* published the first instruction notice relative to this new weapon.

In 1940, the weapon was also made by a second manufacturer: Haenel Waffen und Fahradfabrik of Suhl, which was identifiable by the code 122.

Contacts for the manufacture of the weapon by a third manufacturer were also established with the ex-Austrian Steyr-Daimler Puch Company, which had been part of the Third Reich since the annexation of Austria by the Reich in 1937.

Parachutist firing an MP38. The shape of the magazine housing renders it difficult to handle and forces the shooter to hold the weapon by the magazine, which is always a source of feeding incidents. *Wolf Riess*

A disassembled EMP 36. Note the telescopic tubes designed to protect the recoil spring and the hook placed under the muzzle of the barrel to secure firing through loopholes. *Photo by Michael Heidler*

The MP38 submachine gun adopted on June 29, 1938, by the *Wehrmacht* was at the time the most modern regulation machine gun in the world due to its folding butt, its construction using synthetic materials, and its ERMA breech where the recoil spring is contained in a telescopic tube.

The frame of an MP38.

Comparison between: left, a grip plate of an MP38. On the right for an MP40. Above grip plates showing their screws and the small cylindrical brace in bakelite which goes around the screw.

The aluminum cast grip of an MP38.

Magazine housing made in machined steel and lightened by a circular opening typical of the MP38. The MP38 was delivered originally with a hook shaped bolt handle breech. Some were retrofitted during the war by replacing this piece with a two-piece assembly cocking handle.

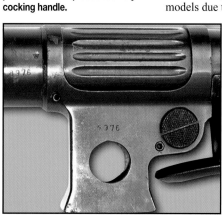

However, it seems that Steyr never produced the MP38. This firm would start to directly produce the MP40, a lighter version of the MP38 from 1940.

When Germany attacked Poland in September 1939, it only had 8,700 MP38 weapons at its disposal. The MP38 therefore only appears very rarely in photographs of the period which more often show German combatants armed with modified MP18/I, MP28/II, and EMP or MP35/I. In addition, it is likely that the secrecy still surrounding the weapon at that time incited the censor to reject photos where it appeared until war was declared.

Examining photos from the beginning of the war, the MP38 appears in photos from 1940 in the hands of paratroopers (*Fallschirmjäger*) and members of the armored (*panzer*) divisions, who were the first to receive the new submachine guns.

The total number of MP38s made probably never exceeded 40,000. All bear either the code "27" for those delivered by ERMA, or "122" for the weapons from Haenel.

Presentation

The MP38 is a 9 mm Parabellum caliber submachine gun operated by non-fixed open breech firing.

The weapon, with no fire mode selector, is operated for continuous burst fire only.

The fairly slow rate of fire allows a trained user to release single shots by releasing pressure on the trigger between each shot.

Because of its folding butt under the weapon, the MP38 was clearly distinguishable from all the other submachine guns built previously by its compactness.

Its design was also very different from previous models due to the presence of a pistol grip and a bolt handle situated on the left side. While previous submachine guns were used in the manner of a carbine: handguard held by the left hand while the right operated the magazine changes, arming the breech, and the action on the trigger, the MP38 had a similar philosophy of use to that of the pistol: the right hand holds the pistol grip and actions the trigger and the left carries out other operations. Initially, it was planned that the user would wear the sling of the weapon crossways meaning his shoulder

supported the weight of the weapon. Photographs taken during operations in the Second World War show combatants frequently ignoring this procedure and holding the weapon in both hands, the sling on the side.

The sight, composed of a fixed leaf graduated for a firing distance of 100 meters and a folding leaf for firing at 200 meters, is evidence of a return to a close quarter combat weapon as for the MP18/I. The rectangular foresight is protected by a tunnel shaped part.

The magazine catch lever is also placed on the left of the magazine housing. The user (mostly right handed at the time) therefore keeps the right hand on the pistol grip while the left hand replaces the magazines and rearms the breech.

A small block, called a "barrel brace," is found under the front part of the barrel. This addition is designed to push the weapon through the openings on armored vehicles and the protuberance at its extremity was meant to prevent the accidental return of the muzzle of the weapon to the inside of the vehicle during fire. At the front of the foresight is a notched ring and the loosening of the screw is slowed down by a spring catch. This ring protects the threaded muzzle used for fixing a blank firing device.

MP38 submachine gun with other objects from the
beginning of the war. *Collection of the Royal Army
Museum of Brussels, photo by Marc de Fromont*

Marking on an MP38 made by ERMA (code 27), 1940.

Serial number on a Haenel made MP38, stamped with the marking "Eagle/37" attributed to this factory.

Serial number on the barrel.

After the adoption of the buffer pitot in rubber, the fixation hooks were removed from the base of the foresight on some MP38 weapons.

The linings of "smooth" magazines were very vulnerable to having depressions in the surface, which stopped the cartridges from moving up and caused feeding difficulties.

On the MP38 and the very first MP40s, a hook positioned forward of the base of the foresight was used to fix a metal buffer pitot. These devices, not without danger if they were not removed before opening fire, were rapidly replaced by rubber-made ones. When the latter were adopted, the hook at the base of the foresight was no longer mounted and a circular groove was machined in the notched ring to strengthen their position at the end of the barrel.

At its rear part, the barrel had a hexagonal screw nut which screwed on the receiver and ensured it could be fixed on the weapon. Two half-rings ensured the centering of the weapon and a safety ring prevents the bolt from unscrewing.

The barrel screw held in place a ring with a hoop through which the weapon sling was passed. This hoop could be positioned either on the right or left side. As standard it was on the left.

The receiver is composed of a steel tube lightened by means of longitudinal grooves. It has on the left side a guideway in which the bolt handle slides.

The guideway has a notch at the rear in which the shooter can block the bolt handle, thereby preventing any accidental forward movement: a rudimentary, but relatively effective, safety system which appeared on the first MP18/I weapons and was to be subsequently copied by very many submachine guns of all nationalities.

At its front part, the receiver is enclosed by the component bearing the magazine housing at its lower part. This component is pierced with a circular cut. The ejection port is on the right side of the weapon.

The weapon is fed by a 32-round magazine; this figure corresponds to the content of two boxes of German army pistol ammunition.

The 16 cartridges contained in each box corresponded to the content of two P.08 or P.38 magazines or a submachine gun half magazine. Boxes of fifty rounds were also available at unit level.

The cartridges were placed in two interlocking piles which met in a half way position at the top of the magazine, in such a way that the upper cartridge was constantly presented in the axis of the barrel. This arrangement led to numerous firing incidents because, in certain magazines, the movement of two columns into one meant it was often blocked if there was even a slight increase in friction engendered by a foreign body or a malformation of the magazine.

This design of the magazine rendered manual loading difficult and required the use of a loading device. This device was supplied to each user of a submachine gun and was kept in a solid pocket on the inside of the left magazine pouch.

The body in which the trigger mechanism is housed is made of bent and welded sheet metal, pierced through with circular cuts to lighten the weapon. It is protected by a handguard in bakelite.

The receiver ends at the rear with a cylindrical buffer pitot solid with the body and on which the model of the weapon, the manufacturer's code, and the year of manufacture is engraved. The serial number is stamped on the left side of the buffer pitot of the receiver.

The pistol grip in cast aluminum is at the rear of the receiver and protected by a black coating which, when worn away, takes on an orange or gold tone.

At its upper part, the grip has a sling loop. The magazine well is at its lower part. A screw bearing a counter-screw fixes the grip to the body of the weapon.

Right at the back of the grip is the metallic butt hinge and its bolt where the lever is on the left side.

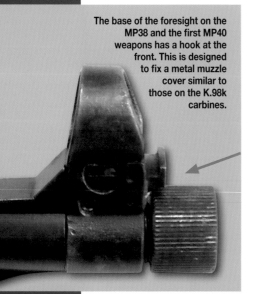

The base of the foresight on the MP38 and the first MP40 weapons has a hook at the front. This is designed to fix a metal muzzle cover similar to those on the K.98k carbines.

A disassembled MP38: the weapon was extremely simple to maintain, as it could be easily and quickly separated into four sub-units: barrel/receiver, mobile breech, recoil spring/ firing pin and grip.

Comparison of Characteristics of the MP38, MP40, and MP41			
	MP38	MP40	MP41
Caliber	9 mm	9 mm	9 mm
Cartridge	9 mm Parabellum (Pistolenpatrone 08)	9 mm Parabellum (Pistolenpatrone 08)	9 mm Parabellum (Pistolenpatrone 08)
Length unfolded butt	83.3 cm	83.3 cm	86 cm
Length folded butt	62.5 cm	62.5 cm	
Barrel length	25 cm	25 cm	25 cm
Empty weight	4.2 kg	4 kg	3.7 kg
Loaded weight	4.7 kg	4.5 kg	4.3 kg
Sight	2 leaves 100 m and 200 m	2 leaves 100 m and 200 m	2 leaves 100 m and 200 m
Magazine capacity	32	32	32
Operation	Open bolt firing, non-fixed breech	Open bolt firing, non-fixed breech	Open bolt firing, non-fixed breech
Possibility to select fire mode	No	No	Yes
Rate of fire	500 shots per minute	500 shots per minute	500 shots per minute

German soldier armed with an MP38 and a magazine pouch with six compartments.

When the bolt handle is engaged in the safety notch the open ejection port can let in foreign bodies.

Grip plates are fixed on both sides, also in bakelite. The mobile breech slides inside the receiver which has a hook shaped bolt handle on its left side and extends to the rear of three telescopic tubes of decreasing length containing the recoil spring, at the front part of which the firing pin is housed.

Because of this design, the weapon is very easy to disassemble and the fact that the recoil spring remains permanently in its telescopic tube unit prevents it from twisting or becoming affected by foreign bodies.

A Failed Hope

The MP38 had a very reasonable level of accuracy for a submachine gun, was easy to control due to its weight and slow rate of fire, and was very easy to handle thanks to its pistol grip and folding butt.

Its modern and compact appearance rendered it very popular with users. However, enthusiasm was lost following some accidents resulting in involuntary firing caused by the backward movement of the breech when the weapon when was dropped.

The reliability of the weapon concerning its operation was also criticized: foreign bodies entering through the open ejection port caused the breech to jam and the magazines caused frequent feeding incidents when they were soiled by foreign bodies or were malformed.

At the beginning of the war, when the *Wehrmacht* confronted armies that had no submachine guns, the MP38 bought a clear advantage to German soldiers in close quarter combat and in skirmishes in no man's land during the "phony war."

Subsequently, when the German army was confronted by better equipped adversaries, this advantage disappeared and many German combatants were forced to replace their MP40 with a more reliable Russian or Italian submachine gun.

On the MP38 (and on the first MP40), the serial number is stamped on the left side of the body. The Eagle 280 stamp of the ERMA factory weapons inspector and the last three figures of the serial number are stamped on the handguard and the top of the grip plate. The arrow indicates the slot in which the breech cocking handle must be blocked so as not to run the risk of letting off an unexpected burst of fire if the weapon is dropped or entangled. The adoption of the cocking handle lever would reduce this risk.

Unearthed several years ago in Normandy, France, this unit is composed of an MP38 magazine housing mounted on an MP40 receiver. Most likely an end-of-war assembly.

Close-up of the lightening grooves machined in the receiver of an MP38 and also the markings on the parts.

CHAPTER 8

THE MP40

Comparison between markings of an MP38 and an MP40 made by Haenel in 1940. Unlike the MP38, on the MP40 only the last two numbers of the year of manufacture appear.

In 1941, the *Waffenamt* adopted letter codes to replace the number codes: "fxo" replaced "122" previously assigned to the Haenel company.

1943 marking with no mention of the manufacturer.

Following the Polish, Belgian, Dutch, and French campaigns, the MP38 had shown proof of its qualities but also its flaws.

The *Wehrmacht* wished to make the weapon general issue by supplying it to all its troops and thereby replacing the dissimilar submachine guns (MP 18, MP28, MP34(ö), MP35, EMP) that they were using.

ERMA was requested to develop a simplified version, made from mostly pressed steel parts. Thus, the MP40 was born, a weapon that was identical to the MP38 on the outside. Because of this, the MP40 cost less than the MP38 (57 *Reichsmarks* in 1944 for an MP40, while an MP38 cost 150) but above all it took less time to manufacture: eighteen hours for an MP40, against twenty-nine for an MP38.

The MP40 started being made at Haenel and ERMA and also at a third manufacturer: Steyr Daimler Puch which was assigned the code 660.

MP40 Manufacturers and Their Codes

During 1940, the German army changed the coding system designed to hide the origin of its equipment from the enemy.

The principle of one, two, or three-figure codes, in use up to that point, was replaced by a two- or three-letter codes in small letters:

- code "27," assigned to ERMA, was abandoned in 1940 in favor of the letter code "ayf"

- code "122" of the Haenel factory was also replaced in 1940 by the letter code "fxo"

- code "660" initially assigned to Steyr was replaced by the code "bnz" in 1941

These three manufacturers produced a total of around a million MP38 and MP40 weapons.

Sub-contractors, who then supplied the main factory, have codes that are identifiable on some parts.

A large number of grips were supplied by the Mers-Werke factory (code: "cos"); the ERMA factory supplied a large number of cocking handles marked with the code: "ayf." These handles were sent to the front as spare parts and were mounted equally on all the MP38 or MP40 weapons by the regimental armorers, wherever the weapon had been made.

Variations in the Manufacture of the MP40

From 1940 to when manufacture was suspended in 1944, the MP40 underwent several developments.

Magazine housing. The magazine housing of the first MP40s was completely smooth. Made from folded and welded metal, the MP40 magazine housing showed itself to be less resistant to impacts relatively quickly compared to the MP38, which was made from machined steel.

The impacts led to malformations which meant the magazine could not be introduced into the weapon and therefore rendered it completely unusable.

Marking on an MP40 made by Steyr (code "660" in 1940).

Code "bnz" replaced the number code "660" on this 1941 made MP40.

An "ayf" 1943 marking on an MP40 made in the last year of manufacture at ERMA. The grip had been made by the Merz-Werle sub-contractor whose "cos" code can be seen on the photo.

Depending on the period and the manufacturer, the letter following the number is either in Latin or Gothic script.

Marking "bnz 43" in the longitudinal axis on an MP40 with a fixed grip corresponding to the last Steyr 1943 makes where the grip is in fact welded to the body.

"Eagle 280" stamp, under the barrel, from the *Waffenamt* office of the Erma factory.

Military proof stamp (A) on the barrel of a Steyr made MP40. The small stamp "Eagle 623"(B) on the ring bearing the sling fixation point.

"Eagle 623" stamp and logo with the code "bnz" of the Steyr Daimler Puch factory, the logo in a shield also featured under the barrel of this MP40.

"Eagle 37" stamp of the inspection office of the *Waffenamt* set up in the Haenel factory. This stamp is also found on the main parts of the weapon and on the magazine made by this factory. The number is a casting number of the barrel and is not connected to the serial number of the weapon.

Code "ayf 42" on an ERMA made MP40.

In 1941 a new type of housing, with its rigidity strengthened by a series of five parallel ribs, was adopted. Some collectors have mistakenly christened this version MP38/40: this name is erroneous as there were only MP38 and MP40 weapons and never an MP38/40.

Bolt handle. The bolt handle breech with hook with no blocking system ran the risk of a sudden backward movement of the breech when the weapon fell on the butt. This backward movement, insufficient to hook the breech on the trigger, could however sometimes bring about chambering then firing of a cartridge when the breech moved forward.

This type of incident gave rise to numerous accidents with submachine guns used by different fighters throughout the Second World War.

It was therefore recommended to carry the weapon with the breech armed and hooked in the safety notch, but this had the disadvantage of allowing foreign bodies to enter the mechanism through the ejection port.

In order to be able to carry the weapon breech closed with no risk of accident, the men equipped with an MP40 had leather straps made, which held the breech forward.

During 1941, the *Wehrmacht* adopted a new model of bolt handle, with a lever which engaged in a notch cut in the receiver. When this lever was pushed in, it immobilized the breech in a forward position and in that way prevented accidents due to its accidental movement.

This simple system proved so effective that these replacement bolt handles were distributed to unit armorers with the order to systematically fix them in place of the old handles with a hook and to file the corresponding small cut out in the receiver of weapons to be transformed.

In the commotion of operations, this directive was not fully applied and some MP38 and MP40 weapons ended the war with the original handle with hook intact despite repeated reminders from the ordnance.

Inspection of the breeches of MP40s before assembly at the ERMA factory in 1942. *Michael Heidler*

On the 1940 MP38 and MP40, the serial number figures horizontally on the left side of the receiver. Subsequently it was moved backwards or slightly to the side of the buffer pitot of the breech solid with the grip.

As was customary on German weapons, the real caliber of the weapon appears under the barrel.

The inspection stamp of the *Waffenamt* and the two or three last figures of the weapon serial number appear even on the smallest parts. This criteria is important for those collectors wishing to avoid purchasing weapons reconstituted after the war from disparate parts.

When the metallic butt is folded under the weapon, it remains totally useable but is a lot less bulky than a standard submachine gun in restricted space.

Comparison between a machined magazine housing of an MP38 (recognizable by its circular cut out) and a smooth magazine housing in pressed steel on an MP40.

Bodies of an MP38 (A) and an MP40 (B) seen from below. The main difference lies in the method of manufacture of the grip.

Ribbed magazine housing which appeared late 1940/early 1941.

Foresight base. The MP38 and MP40 made prior to the end of 1940 had a hook at the front of the base of the foresight. This was designed to fix a metal muzzle nut with hinged flap, which was assigned to each submachine gun to prevent foreign bodies from entering the barrel.

This metal cover was abandoned mid-1940 in favor of a simple rubber cap, which presented several advantages: very low cost, more impervious than metal, no risk of damaging the rubber cap if the shooter used his weapon having forgotten to remove the cap.

This last point allowed the progression of the weapon in wet zones of operation without having to worry about wasting time removing the cap before firing. This was eventually standard in different infantry weapons (K.98k carbines, MG34, and MG42 machine guns and assault rifles).

Muzzle screw nut. This part protected the thread of the muzzle designed for the assembly of the blank fire system (*Manöverpatronengërat*).

In its initial form, this nut is grooved throughout its whole length.

Superb example of a production Steyr 1942 (marking "bnz 42"), with the ribbed loader lane, which was typical during this period.

MP40 (bottom) with other submachine guns from the same period which it frequently faced during combat (top to bottom): British army and Resistance Sten Mk.I, Thompson 1928 model, and a Soviet PPSh 41. Despite the criticisms the German soldiers had (tendency to jam, unsatisfactory magazine), the MP40 was a weapon ahead of its time: compact, accurate, and stable during firing and which continued to give good service to its users long after 1945. *Collection of the Royal Army Museum of Brussels, photo by Marc de Fromont*

Until 1941, the breech of the MP40 was equipped with a hook shaped bolt handle (A), as on the MP18, 28, and 38 before. The replacement of this type of handle, which did not allow the immobilization of the breech was ordered in favor of a cocking handle (B) which became blocked in a notch on the receiver so as to stop accidental backward movement of the breech.

Second type of bolt handle. This cocking handle is blocked in a notch on the receiver. When the handle is free from its safety notch, a zone of red paint (often worn out on weapons seen today) appears through the small circular window pierced at the top of the handle.

While waiting for the replacement cocking handles to be put at the disposal of regimental armorers, the technical notices of the German army recommended the use of leather straps (generally re-cut from old K.98k or MP40 slings) to maintain the breech in forward position on the MP40 fitted with a hook shaped cocking handle.

Cocking handle in locked position, this prevents any accidental backward movement of the breech.

After the adoption of the rubber muzzle cap, the notched bolt protecting the threading of the muzzle was grooved in its central part (A) to strengthen the hold of the muzzle cap, whereas on certain weapons already fitted with a hook, this was removed (B).

After the adoption of the rubber muzzle cap, a new model of screw nut was taken up. It is distinguishable from the initial model by the presence of a transversal groove designed to favor a better hold of the muzzle cap.

Barrel screw nut. This nut, fixing the barrel to the receiver, was originally hexagonal in shape. This part was replaced by a cylindrical nut with two flat parts to aid tightening at the end, 1942/beginning 1943, as part of a general plan of simplification.

Grip. The aluminum cast grip of the MP38 was to be replaced by a grip made of folded and welded steel on the MP40. This fairly fragile structure had the tendency to get out of place after violent impacts. The makers of the MP40 proposed several types of grips reinforced with strips of metal welded to the inside of the grip frame.

At the beginning of 1943, the Steyr Daimler Puch Company put into service a completely new model of grip, that collectors call "large trigger guard" because of the solid appearance of this part.

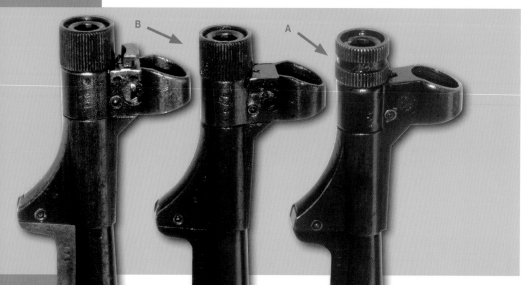

Gebirgsjäger armed with an MP40.

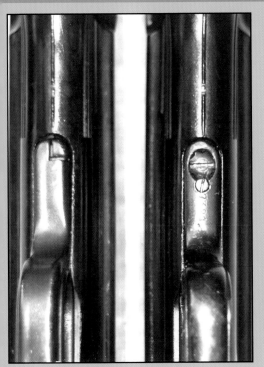

Comparison between the trigger guards of an MP40 with a detachable grip, screwed to the body (right) and a final type MP40 with non-detachable grip welded permanently to the body (left).

Comparison between trigger guard on the first type of grip (A) and the second type (B). The heavy shape of the latter gave rise to the nickname "Large trigger guard MP40." A slight difference in shape between the two grips in the zone where the sling passes can also be noted.

First type of trigger guard reinforced by a strip welded on the interior.

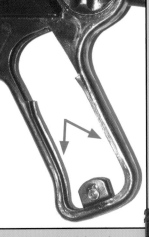

First type of grip reinforced on the inside by a strip of welded metal.

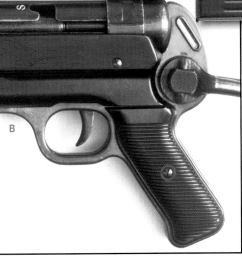

Last version of the MP40, appeared also at Steyr at the end of 1943, where the grip is welded to the body.

This grip, composed of two half shells in pressed metal welded to each other, proved to be very robust. Steyr introduced a final simplification of the MP40: previously the grip was connected to the body by a stud at its upper part and screwed to it in front of the trigger guard.

Steyr conceived a grip simply welded to the body of the weapon. The MP40 with a welded grip represents the last development of the MP40, whose manufacture was to be suspended in 1944 in favor of the MP43 assault rifle.

Body. Several variations can be noted in the method of manufacture of the body. Rather than going into a detailed description, readers can study the photographs in this chapter. Slight variations can also be noted on small parts, axes, etc.

Fixings. Handguard and grip plates. These elements are made from pressure- cast bakelite. The inside of these pieces have symbols representing their origin. A black-brown color originally, these fixings were redder at the end of the war. The final makes show fibers and wood shavings, added to the phenolic resin, a component of bakelite, in order to economize raw materials.

After the war, spare fixings in wood or in cast aluminum would sometimes be mounted in some countries that had put the MP40 back into service in order to replace the broken parts.

Barrel brace. On the MP38 and the first MP40, this part is made in aluminum alloy and sometimes carries the marking "NURAL"; subsequently this brace is made in bakelite. A variation made in pressed metal appeared around 1942.

On this last version the manufacturer's markings and the exit date from the factory are stamped lengthways on the strip welded to the upper part at the rear of the body. The serial number is stamped on the body parallel to this marking.

Magazine bolt lever on an MP40 on a Haenel 1941 made magazine.

Magazine bolt lever on a Steyr 1942 made MP40.

Butt of an MP40 made at the end of 1943: the braces are made of several parts and are fairly crudely welded.

Grip plates in grooved wood replacing those originally in bakelite that were probably broken.

This photo illustrates the difficulty of firing from cover with a submachine fitted with a long vertical magazine: the shooter is dangerously exposed when aiming at the target.

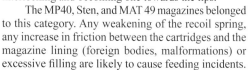

Barrel rest bar in cast in aluminum alloy marked "Nural." This type is seen more on MP38 and early made MP40 weapons.

Magazines. The magazines were generally one of the main sources of malfunction of automatic weapons. This is especially true for those on submachine guns with magazines extrapolated from the model covered by the Schmeisser patent which has two cartridge columns interlocking and becoming one towards the lips.

The MP40, Sten, and MAT 49 magazines belonged to this category. Any weakening of the recoil spring, any increase in friction between the cartridges and the magazine lining (foreign bodies, malformations) or excessive filling are likely to cause feeding incidents.

The first MP38 and MP40 magazines have smooth sides which are easily dented on impact. They were the cause of many operational problems.

A new type of magazine with sides with two grooves was adopted from 1941.

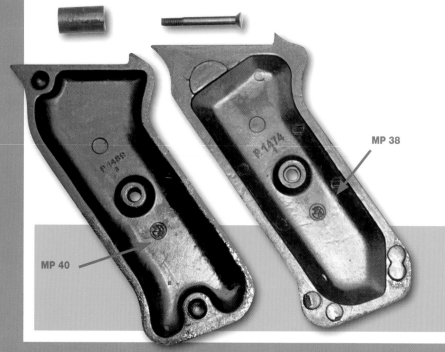

MP 38

MP 40

Straight grip plate of an MP38 and an MP40: the difference in shape means that the two types are not interchangeable. Above: the small cylinder in bakelite is placed around the screw holding the grip plates and is used to reinforce their central part.

MP 38 and MP40 with a P.38 pistol,
a model 24 stick grenade, and several
personal objects of German soldiers.
*Collection of the Royal Army Museum
of Brussels, photo by Marc de Fromont*

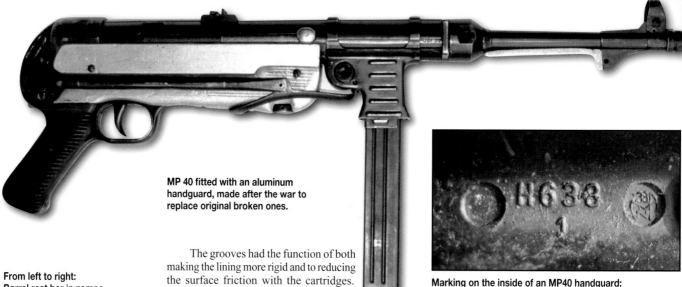

MP 40 fitted with an aluminum handguard, made after the war to replace original broken ones.

From left to right:
Barrel rest bar in zamac (zinc alloy)
Barrel rest bar in bakelite
Barrel rest bar in pressed steel which appears (although not always systematically) on makes after 1942

The grooves had the function of both making the lining more rigid and to reducing the surface friction with the cartridges. They were not perfect but these magazines were satisfactory and remained in service until the end of the war.

The MP38 and MP40 magazines have a hole situated opposite marker 32, corresponding to the maximum capacity of the magazine. This orifice,

Marking on the inside of an MP40 handguard: number and circular identification symbol.

facilitating the entry of foreign bodies, meant that it was often covered by welding tin over the hole by users of the MP40 operating in sandy areas. It was simply removed on the MP40 magazines that were made to order for the French army after 1945.

MP40 Accessories

Blank firing device. This is a long pointed rod with a calibrated orifice inserted into the barrel where it is held in position by a threaded ring which screws on the threads of the muzzle. This system allows the weapon to function with bursts of fire with the blank 9 mm cartridge (Manöverpatrone 08).

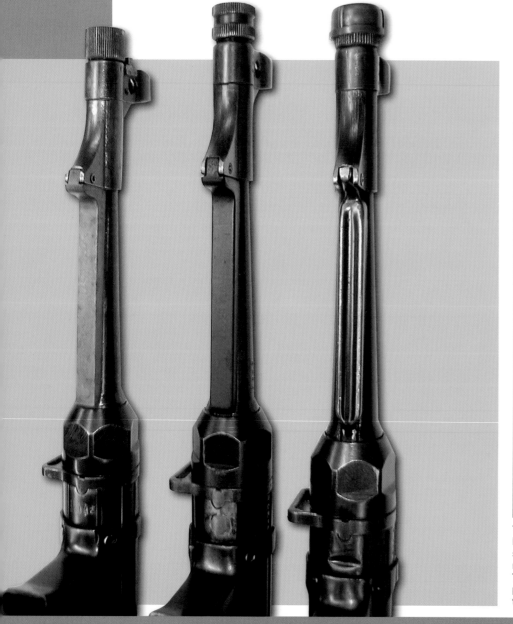

The sling enabling the weapon to be carried conveniently and hands free. Worn cross wise, the weight was supported by the shoulder and meant it could be held by the grip. The other hand remained free to change the magazine or operate the bolt handle. This advantage of handling made the MP38 and MP40 much more popular that the bulky submachine guns with wooden butts such as the MP28/II or MP35/I.

From left to right: a Schmeisser system 20-round magazine for MP18/I, under which is a German box of sixteen Parabellum 9 mm cartridges, an MP40 magazine with smooth sides and an MP40 magazine with ribbed sides. The MP40 magazine is directly derived from the first Schmeisser magazines.

Six-compartment magazine pouch in olive green canvas. *Hermann Historica*

122 – Haenel 1940 manufacture

agp – Eisenwerke manufacture G. Meuer 1940

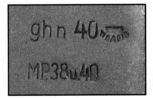

ghn – Auer Gesellschaft 1940 manufacture

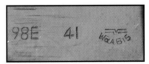

98E – Steyr 1941 manufacture

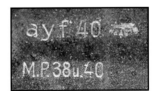

ayf – Erma 1940 manufacture

They seem to have only been made in restricted numbers and are extremely rare today. Even the German regulation blank cartridge was quite rare.

On the other hand, the market is teeming with false blank firing muzzle caps as well as various muzzle systems (flash concealer, barrel nuts, etc.).

Magazine brush. Every soldier of the *Wehrmacht* was supplied with an RG34 (*Reinigungsgerät modell 1934*) cleaning kit. For users of the MP40, this RG 34 was completed with a 21 mm diameter brush which, attached to a chain pull-through of the barrel contained in the RG34, was used to clean the inside of the magazines. The disassembly and the cleaning of the magazines were indispensable to eliminate dust and foreign bodies which could cause feeding incidents.

Magazine loading tool. The Schmeisser type magazine which equipped the MP40 (just like its British copy: the Sten magazine) was difficult to load by hand with more than fifteen cartridges. The user of an MP40 therefore had to use a device to facilitate loading. This indispensable item is carried in a special pocket in the left of the magazine pouch.

Apart from the factories producing the MP40, ERMA (ayf), Haenel (122 then fxo), Steyr (cure and 98), and several other metallurgical enterprises were also solicited to manufacture them: Franksiche Eisenwerke (bte), Lorch & Hartenberger (gqm).

Magazine pouch. The MP40 was supplied with six magazines. They were placed in two pouches on the belt in a slightly oblique position and are attached by metal rings to the belt suspension slings. The left pocket has a pouch on its external side in which the indispensable loading tool is placed.

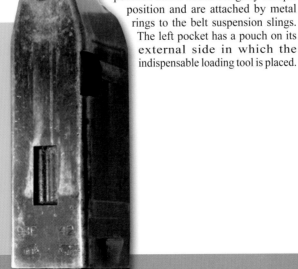

Users of the MP38 and 40 were supplied with a brush for cleaning the inside of the magazine. This brush could be attached to the cleaning chain pull-through contained in the RG34 of the K.98k carbine that the majority of combatants were equipped with.

The movement of two columns into one created mechanical resistance which generated feeding incidents. The adoption of magazines with ribbed sides helped to reduce this problem.

Left: French made post-war magazine produced for the MP40 used by the French army. The parkerized finish and the absence of an orifice and a loading marker enables the identification of this version.

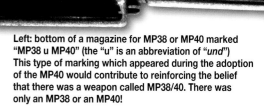

Left: bottom of a magazine for MP38 or MP40 marked "MP38 u MP40" (the "u" is an abbreviation of "und") This type of marking which appeared during the adoption of the MP40 would contribute to reinforcing the belief that there was a weapon called MP38/40. There was only an MP38 or an MP40!

Franksiche Eisenwerke (bte) magazine of 1943.

MP38 magazine made by Haenel in 1939.

Code "27" from the ERMA factory on a magazine made in 1940.

Code "ayf" replacing the numerical code "27" end 1940.

From 1942 Steyr abandoned the code "98E" in favor of the code "kur." The control stamp "Eagle 815" is typical of Steyr Daimler Puch.

A gqm magazine made in 1944 (only the "4" is stamped) by the Lorch & Hartenberger metalwarenfabrik company of Idar-Oberstein.

Another type of magazine pouch containing six magazines and fitted with a pocket for the loading tool was also supplied. This model was worn cross wise due to its large belt. The information currently available does not allow us to determine if the magazine pouches with six compartments were the initial pouch of the MP38 or not. The fact that it appears frequently on photos of parachutists led to the idea that this model had been conceived for them. However, it is possible that the *Fallschirmjäger*, as they were the first to benefit from the first MP38s, were mainly equipped with this early type magazine pouch.

In general the magazine pouches were made in grey-green, beige, or grey-blue canvas. There were also pouches with three compartments made in leather perhaps for the police.

It is important to note that the MP40 pouches with three or six compartments have been copied extensively for several years and some copies, made in the Czech Republic using tools of the period, are almost perfect.

Magazine pouches in brown textured leather that were made for the Norwegian army post-war, are also found on the market, as well as another model with four compartments which are of Yugoslavian origin.

Strangley, until 1942 Steyr used the code 98 E to mark its magazines whereas it would have been more logical to use the code 660 then bnz.

Magazines. For convenience we have chosen to deal with magazines in this chapter even though they are an element of the weapon rather than an accessory.

From 1940 the German army, which had put a considerable amount of captured foreign equipment at the use of its troops, was confronted with such a disparity of material that it took the decision to mark the military magazines in order to facilitate the identification of the type of weapon to which it corresponded (MP 35/I and EMP magazines generally avoided this measure).

Apart from the manufacturer's code, the last two figures of the date and the *Waffenamt* stamp, the first MP38 magazines were not marked. From 1940, the marking MP38 u. 40 (MP 38 and 40), was stamped on the base of the magazine to indicate which type of weapon they matched.

The manufacturer's code and the last two figures of the year of manufacture were stamped at the rear of the MP38 and MP40 magazines.

Sling. The MP40 was fitted with a sling in crisscrossed leather with a slide similar to those on the K.98k slings, with two holes (whereas there are three on the K.98k and Sturmgewehr slings) at one end used to close on a metal dowel. This sling passed around the neck meant the user had great freedom of movement. At the end of the war the "*Ersatz*" slings made in fabric and with leather ends were put into service.

To try to equal the fire power of the Soviet PPSh 41 submachine gun, equipped with a 71-round drum magazine, the Germans tried the 40/I weapon fed by two 32-round magazines with a slide system allowing the cartridges to be positioned in turn. *Collection of the Royal Army Museum of Brussels, photo by Marc de Fromont*

Left and center: two Israeli-made MP40 slings recognizable by their brass buckle marked with a letter in Hebrew and right: an Italian sling in smooth, light brown leather, identical to the pre-1945 German slings.

Rare photo showing a member of a Russian tank crew proudly displaying an MP40 fitted with a silencer.

Protective cover. A canvas protective cover allowed soldiers operating in sandy conditions to protect the mechanism of their weapon from foreign bodies. We can see today thick, webbing type covers offered on the market for a submachine gun and several magazines. They are made for collectors and tend to be fanciful and Indian-made.

Winter trigger. This accessory, extrapolated from the one that had been developed for the K.98k carbine, is composed of two half shells which are placed on either side of the trigger guard (not unlike our modern trigger guard lock) and assembled by a clip.

Silencer. In February 1943 the *Heeres Waffenamt* asked the Arado, Brandenburg and Schneider-Opel firms to carry out research for a silencer for an MP40. The fixing of this accessory is quite easy due to the presence of threads at the muzzle. The operation of a weapon firing with open breech could scarcely be silent, but a silencer could at least render the weapon inaudible at a medium distance or make it difficult to locate.

Major Heilmeier, in charge of testing, established a report on the February 13, 1943, stating that this silencer, copied from a Russian one, had rubber diaphragms. This principle was kept because even though it was less effective at deadening the sound compared with silencers with metallic baffles, it retained better accuracy during firing.

An MP40 canvas protection cover here worn in North Africa by a paratrooper.

The total number of MP38s and MP40s made by the three factories involved in the production is estimated to be between 800,000 and 1,100,000. The last weapons seem to have been delivered by Steyr in October 1944. The deliveries in 1943 and 1944 include a good number of Beretta 38/42, and those of 1945 are essentially made up of MP3008 and other copies of Sten, as well as all types of sub machine guns assembled at the last minute from spare parts that were still available in German factories.

Production of the MP40							
	1939	1940	1941	1942	1943	1944	1945
Heer	5700	95,100	139,667	151,033	220,572	217,614*	85,689*
Kriegsmarine				12,500	3,776	2,081	0
Luftwaffe				66,300	9,973	6,244	0

* The figures for 1945 could vary because it most likely concerned MP40 and MP38 weapons. It is also possible that submachine guns of foreign origin used by the *Wehrmacht* were included in the figure. In any case, the disorganization of the armed services was such that the figures mentioned are not reliable.

Disassembly of the MP40

1 Press the magazine bolt lever to extract the magazine

2 Pull back the breech and check there is no cartridge in the chamber, then carry out a safety shot by pointing the weapon in a safe direction

3 Pull down the disassembly button positioned under the handguard and make a 90° turn in either direction

4 Carry out a 45° rotation to the receiver while holding the grip then separate the receiver from the body

5 Move the bolt handle back to remove the breech and the recoil unit from the receiver

6 Separate the breech from the recoil spring

7 Basic disassembly of an MP40. The ordinary field disassembly is limited to the points mentioned above. The firing pin which should appear at the forward of the recoil unit has been removed during deactivation on this weapon

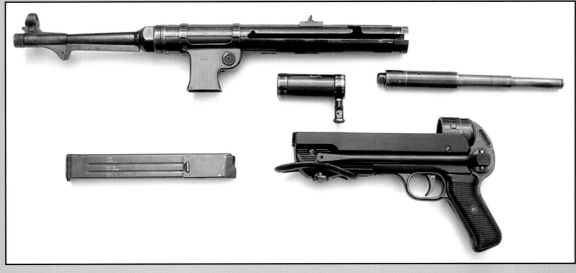

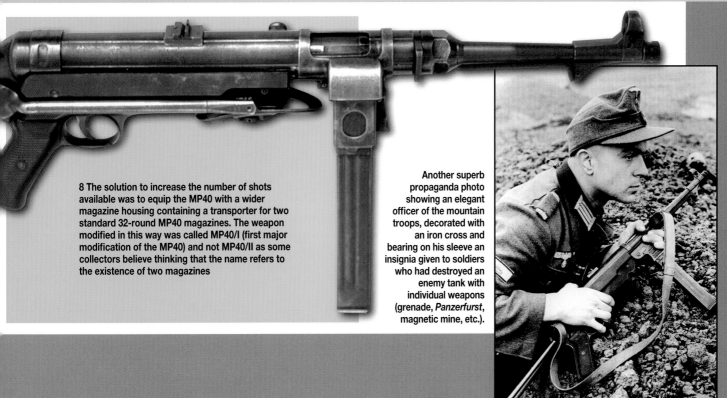

8 The solution to increase the number of shots available was to equip the MP40 with a wider magazine housing containing a transporter for two standard 32-round MP40 magazines. The weapon modified in this way was called MP40/I (first major modification of the MP40) and not MP40/II as some collectors believe thinking that the name refers to the existence of two magazines

Another superb propaganda photo showing an elegant officer of the mountain troops, decorated with an iron cross and bearing on his sleeve an insignia given to soldiers who had destroyed an enemy tank with individual weapons (grenade, *Panzerfurst*, magnetic mine, etc.).

MP40 fitted with safety block by the German police. *Dr. Pierre Blaise*

Member of the police regiment firing an MP40 fitted with a *"Blocksicherung." Bundesarchiv*

Example fitted with a widened magazine housing including a removable double magazine compartment. This part could be mounted on any MP40 to replace the original magazine housing. The examples concerned were MP40s made by Steyr Daimler Puch or Erman and dated 1941 or 1942. *Musée 1939–45, Roscoff, France*

Two Rare Variations: The MP40/I and the MP40 With Safety Block

The MP40/I. German soldiers complained of being disadvantaged in close quarter combat when confronted with Soviet combatants. The Germans were armed with 32-round magazines on their MP38 and MP40s and the Soviets had PPSh 41 submachine guns with a 71-round drum magazine.

Many of them got rid of their supplied issued weapon in favor of a PPSh 41 taken from the enemy, a situation which brought into question the superiority of German technology.

This led to the experimentation of an MP40 fitted with a widened magazine housing in which two magazines were held mounted on a slide which enabled the rapid replacement of the first magazine, when empty, by the second.

This weapon, designated under the name MP40/I (MP 40/ first modification), showed itself to be too heavy and impractical and therefore the project was not completed.

In France, for several years now collectors have been able to admire a superb MP40/I in the Musée de l'Armée in Paris. Another specimen can be seen in the Memorial Museum in Bayeux in the Calvados. The example, photos of which appear in this article, was given to the Royal Army Museum in Brussels by an anonymous donor.

Detail of the safety which blocks the breech in a forward position. *Dr. Pierre Blaise*

The Police MP40 with safety block. The German police were not particularly spoiled when it came to their supply of MP40 weapons and often had to settle for older models [MP 18/I, MP28/II, EMP, MP35/I, and principally the MP34(ö)]. However, several MP40s were supplied to the police before the second model of cocking handle came into service. To prevent incidents caused by the accidental recoil of the breech, the police fitted a safety block on their weapons. Considering the small number of MP40s used by the police, the MP40 with safety block is today a rare type of submachine gun. As on the other submachine guns used by the police, a small police reception stamp (Eagle /L, Eagle/C, or Eagle/E) was sometimes, but not always, stamped on the weapons.

The presence of a widened magazine housing and two magazines interferes with the handling capacity and the balance of the weapon. *Collection of the Royal Army Museum of Brussels, photo by Marc de Fromont*

Three submachine guns, an LP42 pistol, and a 1939 model "Egg" grenade, with accessories used by the German security forces. *Collection of the Royal Army Museum of Brussels, photo by Marc de Fromont*

The MP40, a Legendary Weapon

The MP40 had made a very strong impression on those French combatants that used it. French soldiers that had come across it in 1939 during skirmishes in "No Man's Land" complained of not being equipped with a similar type of weapon, so marvelously adapted to patrols and surprise attacks.

After the defeat of 1940, the French-occupied population had of course noticed these short and easy to handle weapons that were so different from the long Lebel and Berthier 07-15 rifles that French troops were so often armed with at the start of the war.

The image of the MP40 was intensely exploited by German propaganda which photographed more willingly the bearers of MG34 and MP40 than soldiers equipped with the traditional K.98k carbine. The magnificent photos of the period in the book by G. de Vries and BJ Martens well illustrate the visual appeal that the weapon had for the correspondents of the German military press (PK).

Later, the MP40, as the symbol of a young and aggressive weapon, continued to hold a place of pride in occupied Europe where the weapon figured prominently in recruitment posters for the *Waffen-SS*.

Despite the entry into service of more modern weapons, the prestige of the MP40 remained intact at the end of the war and many allied soldiers and resistance fighters hurried to swap their supplied weapon for an MP40 when they had the opportunity of capturing one!

For all that, was the weapon exceptional? Definitely not, it was undeniably a very good weapon, but it was not perfect.

Its principle qualities were:

*   its compactness and handling ability strengthened by the presence of a pistol grip and a folding butt.

*   the accuracy of its fire, accurate to a distance of 200 meters and the ease of handling during continuous burst fire.

*   the ease of disassembly due to the spring housed in a telescopic tube.

Concerning its negative points:

*   the delicate operation of the magazines, the cause of jamming when they were malformed or dirty.

*   jamming arising from foreign bodies entering via the ejection port.

*   a practical hold for the dominant hand but fairly inconvenient for the weak hand which could not hold it satisfactorily. The shape of the magazine housing meant it could not be used as a grip, it is not possible to hold the weapon by the barrel devoid of a protective jacket without burning the hands after the firing of several bursts.

Photos of the period often show shooters simply holding the handguard with the left hand in a position similar to that when firing a small caliber carbine (which was possible by the moderate recoil and weight of the weapon). Once upright, the use of the sling used crosswise and the pistol grip meant for an easier handling of the weapon.

The bulkiness of the long magazine positioned under the barrel was an obstruction during firing in the prone position or from behind shelter: to take aim, the shooter has to expose the top part of his body to enemy fire.

After the Second World War, the MP40s retrieved from European soil were put back into service by armies re-formed after the war: the French army supplied its parachutist, and naval commandoes with it and would go on to use it extensively in the Indochina War.

The Czech, Polish, Austrian, East German, and Israeli armies and police would use the MP40 extensively up until the 1950s. The last official user of the MP40 was the Norwegian army which did not declassify these weapons until after 1980.

At the end of the Indochina War, the French army was on the receiving end of the MP40, in the hands of Algerian rebels. These weapons, coming from former *Wehrmacht* stocks, were delivered to the FLN by German traffickers or by weapons manufacturers in communist countries.

As much for its own qualities as well as the symbolic qualities bestowed on it by the Third Reich, the MP40 was a trophy much prized by Allied soldiers. Here, an infantryman in a Jeep showing a captured MP40 to an envious bomber crew from the US Army Air Force. *Michael Heidler*

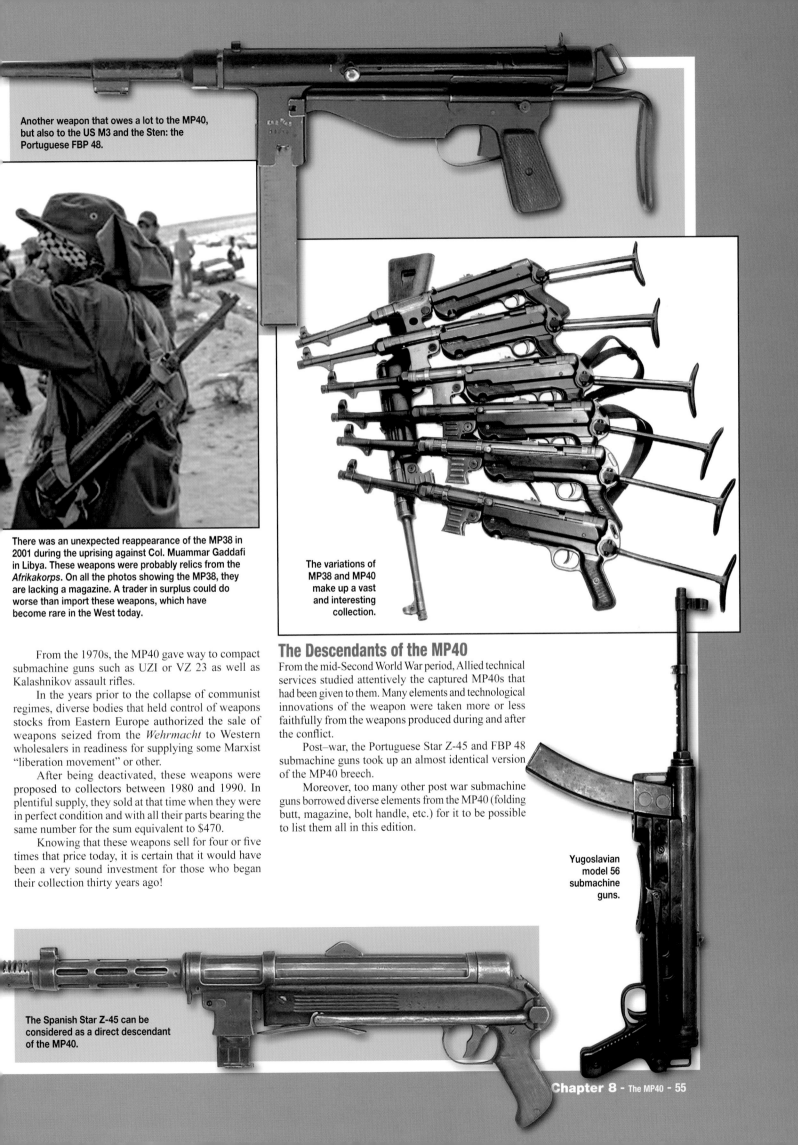

Another weapon that owes a lot to the MP40, but also to the US M3 and the Sten: the Portuguese FBP 48.

There was an unexpected reappearance of the MP38 in 2001 during the uprising against Col. Muammar Gaddafi in Libya. These weapons were probably relics from the *Afrikakorps*. On all the photos showing the MP38, they are lacking a magazine. A trader in surplus could do worse than import these weapons, which have become rare in the West today.

The variations of MP38 and MP40 make up a vast and interesting collection.

From the 1970s, the MP40 gave way to compact submachine guns such as UZI or VZ 23 as well as Kalashnikov assault rifles.

In the years prior to the collapse of communist regimes, diverse bodies that held control of weapons stocks from Eastern Europe authorized the sale of weapons seized from the *Wehrmacht* to Western wholesalers in readiness for supplying some Marxist "liberation movement" or other.

After being deactivated, these weapons were proposed to collectors between 1980 and 1990. In plentiful supply, they sold at that time when they were in perfect condition and with all their parts bearing the same number for the sum equivalent to $470.

Knowing that these weapons sell for four or five times that price today, it is certain that it would have been a very sound investment for those who began their collection thirty years ago!

The Descendants of the MP40

From the mid-Second World War period, Allied technical services studied attentively the captured MP40s that had been given to them. Many elements and technological innovations of the weapon were taken more or less faithfully from the weapons produced during and after the conflict.

Post–war, the Portuguese Star Z-45 and FBP 48 submachine guns took up an almost identical version of the MP40 breech.

Moreover, too many other post war submachine guns borrowed diverse elements from the MP40 (folding butt, magazine, bolt handle, etc.) for it to be possible to list them all in this edition.

Yugoslavian model 56 submachine guns.

The Spanish Star Z-45 can be considered as a direct descendant of the MP40.

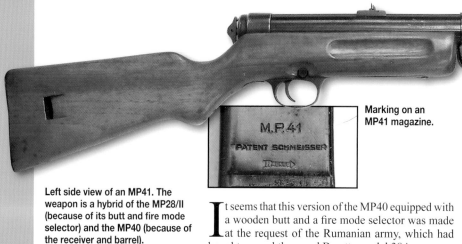

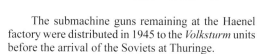

Marking on an MP41 magazine.

Left side view of an MP41. The weapon is a hybrid of the MP28/II (because of its butt and fire mode selector) and the MP40 (because of the receiver and barrel).

Commercial marking featuring on the top of an MP41 receiver.

Device for loading the magazine marked MP41 and Haenel.

It seems that this version of the MP40 equipped with a wooden butt and a fire mode selector was made at the request of the Rumanian army, which had bought several thousand Beretta model 38A weapons and appreciated the submachine guns conceived as small carbines and having a selective fire capacity.

The adaptation of the MP40 was realized by Hugo Schmeisser within the C.G. Haenel company where he was technical director. To make the MP41, Schmeisser settled for blending the butt and the fire mode selector of his MP28/II with certain elements of the MP40 by slightly modifying the breech to allow its hooking on the trigger during single shot fire.

It is a question of a hybrid weapon whose lower part is visibly more the MP28/II and the upper part is more like that of an MP40 with a fixed barrel and devoid of barrel brace.

The weapon had typical commercial markings on the top of the receiver "MP 41 Patent Schmeisser – C.G. Haenel Suhl." Its magazine and magazine reloading tool are also marked MP41 and bear the Haenel logo.

It seems that the manufacture of the MP41 was carried out in two steps: an initial delivery of around 26,000 weapons to Rumania in 1941 and another from 1,000 to 2,000 more, throughout 1944 probably for the German police.

The submachine guns remaining at the Haenel factory were distributed in 1945 to the *Volksturm* units before the arrival of the Soviets at Thuringe.

The MP41 was also used by German police if we consider the evidence of this on certain photos of the period.

Serial number 14400 and *Waffenamt* control stamps on the left side of the weapon.

Scene of a fire during the repression of the Warsaw uprising in 1944. This photo shows a surprising mix of submachine gun models: a Suomi KP31 (A), an MP41 (B), an MP40 (C), and an MP38/II (D).

Comparison between an MP40 and an MP41 breech. The two models are differentiated by the presence of a miniscule lateral groove which enables the passage of the fire mode selector arm (arrow) on the breech of the MP41.

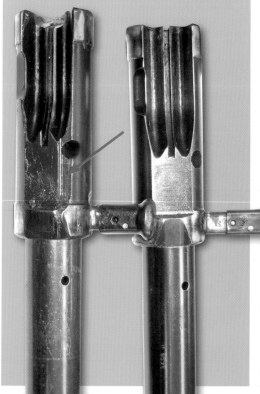

CHAPTER 10

FOREIGN SUBMACHINE GUNS IN THE SERVICE OF THE THIRD REICH

Finnish Suomi KP31 submachine gun. Several hundred were bought before the war by the SS and the specimens made under license in Denmark by Madsen were seized after the invasion of Denmark and integrated into the German arsenal.

At the declaration of war in 1939 the *Wehrmacht*, yet to accomplish its total ascent to power, found itself confronted with a shortage of both equipment and weaponry which was exacerbated throughout the following years by the increase in its numbers.

Despite losses, the number of troops in the *Wehrmacht* went from 5,600,000 men in 1940, to 7,200,000 in 1941 because of the incorporation of new age groups and foreign contingents.

To arm all the combatants and replace weapons damaged during operations was a real feat and the difficulty was further increased by the shortage of raw materials as well as the destruction inflicted on German industry by Allied bombing.

The weapons and ammunition ministry therefore put in place, from the beginning of the war, a policy

Den im Hohen Norden in treuer Waffenbrüderschaft kämpfenden deutschen Truppen werden 120 Stück von dieser Maschinenpistole "Suomi" überreicht.
Marschall von Finnland.
Freiherr Mannerheim.

Silver plaque fixed on the butt of the 120 Finnish submachine guns given by Gustav Mannerheim, the Marshal of Finland, to German soldiers that had fought on the Eastern front with Finnish troops.

of systematic retrieval and return to service of useable captured enemy equipment and undertook weapons purchases abroad from allied countries: Italy, Spain, and Finland.

The *Wehrmacht* used therefore many submachine guns of foreign origin. We will discuss here only regulation weapons used in the *Wehrmacht*, the police, or the *Waffen-SS*.

Outside these entities, there are cases of some German soldiers occasionally using submachine guns captured in the field, without it ever going beyond the level of individual salvage. We can cite the example of the 1928 model Thompson captured from British forces in North Africa with which some soldiers of the *Afrikakorps* were photographed, without including this occasional use to a regulation one.

All the equipment captured by the *Wehrmacht* during these campaigns received an identification code. These codes are listed in the famous identification files of foreign equipment (*Kennblätter Fremdengeräts*).

It is a type of stock catalogue. The mention of any submachine gun on the document indicates that this type of weapon was stocked in a depot of the Third Reich but does not signify that the weapon was put into service in the *Wehrmacht* or another organization, unless perhaps in the ranks of the *Volksturm* during the last weeks of the war when it was necessary to use everything available in men and equipment!

The foreign submachine guns in service in the *Wehrmacht* came from two sources:

1 From orders placed with foreign enterprises (same as for the Suomi and Beretta submachine guns)

SS motorcyclist armed with a Suomi.

38A model Italian Beretta: event though it appears it was not ordered officially, this weapon appears frequently in the hands of German soldiers on photographs of the period.

First version of the grooved barrel of the 38A model, the Beretta 38/42 model was manufactured in large quantity for the *Wehrmacht* by Beretta.

Very simplified markings on the second version of a 38/42 Beretta.

Hallmark on the wooden butt of a 38/42 model.

Marking on a 38/42 model Beretta.

2 Weapons captured during combat, as was the case for the PPSh 41 Russian submachine guns or the British Sten.

Foreign Purchases

Suomi submachine guns. From 1931, Finland exported the excellent KP 31 submachine gun, a regulation weapon in its army.

Before the declaration of war the SS organization, which was in desperate need of weapons to equip its militarized units, ordered several hundred 9 mm caliber Parabellum Suomi from their manufacturer: the Tikkakoski weapons company.

Other Suomi were recovered after the invasion of Denmark where this weapon, made under license by the Madsen company, was regulation issue. Several photos of the period show the Suomi in the hands of the *Waffen-SS*.

Marshal Gustav Mannerheim, Marshal of Finland and head of state, made a personal donation of 120 KP31 weapons to German soldiers that had shown distinguished service during combat alongside Finnish forces.

Beretta submachine guns. The 38A model Beretta submachine guns were highly appreciated by German combatants who discovered its good features during operations in North Africa. From that period the Germans recovered them for their own use whenever they could.

Several accounts from the period show that the Beretta submachine guns, with a magazine where the cartridges presented alternatively on each of the lips, were less likely to jam than the MP38 and MP40 which had Schmeisser type magazines.

In 1942, as the production of the MP40 was not sufficient to cover the needs created by the war on the Eastern front, the weapons ministry ordered a simplified version of the 38 model Beretta: the 38/42 model.

This weapon is different from the 38 model as it is less bulky, has a fixed sight, no barrel jacket and a simplified recoil spring. The Beretta 38/42 barrel is thick, grooved initially, and then smooth on later productions. At the muzzle, two openings oriented towards the top helped to reduce the uplift of the weapon. The Beretta submachine gun has two triggers: the one on the front for single shot fire and at the rear for continuous burst fire.

A German officer armed with a 38A model Beretta writing a message.

In 1943 and 1944, Beretta delivered an average of 20,000 submachine guns per month to the German army.

In 1943, during a conference attended by the *Gauleiters* of the Tyrol and Carinthia, the weapons and munitions minister, Albert Speer, ordered that the responsibility for all questions relative to the weapon and its production be removed from the Italian authorities and placed under his own control.

After the armistice of 1943 was signed between the King of Italy and Marshal Badoglio and the Allies, the Italian forces for the most part supported the new government and from then on fought with the Anglo-American forces.

Only a small quantity of faithful supported the Italian social Republic government which controlled the north part of the country under the authority of Benito Mussolini. This territory was the most industrialized part and where the armaments factories were located.

In addition to the orders placed by the Third Reich with Beretta, the German forces recovered a significant booty of Italian weapons after the armistice of 1943. As soon as this change in alliance was announced, the German forces encircled and disarmed the Italian units whenever they were able to do so.

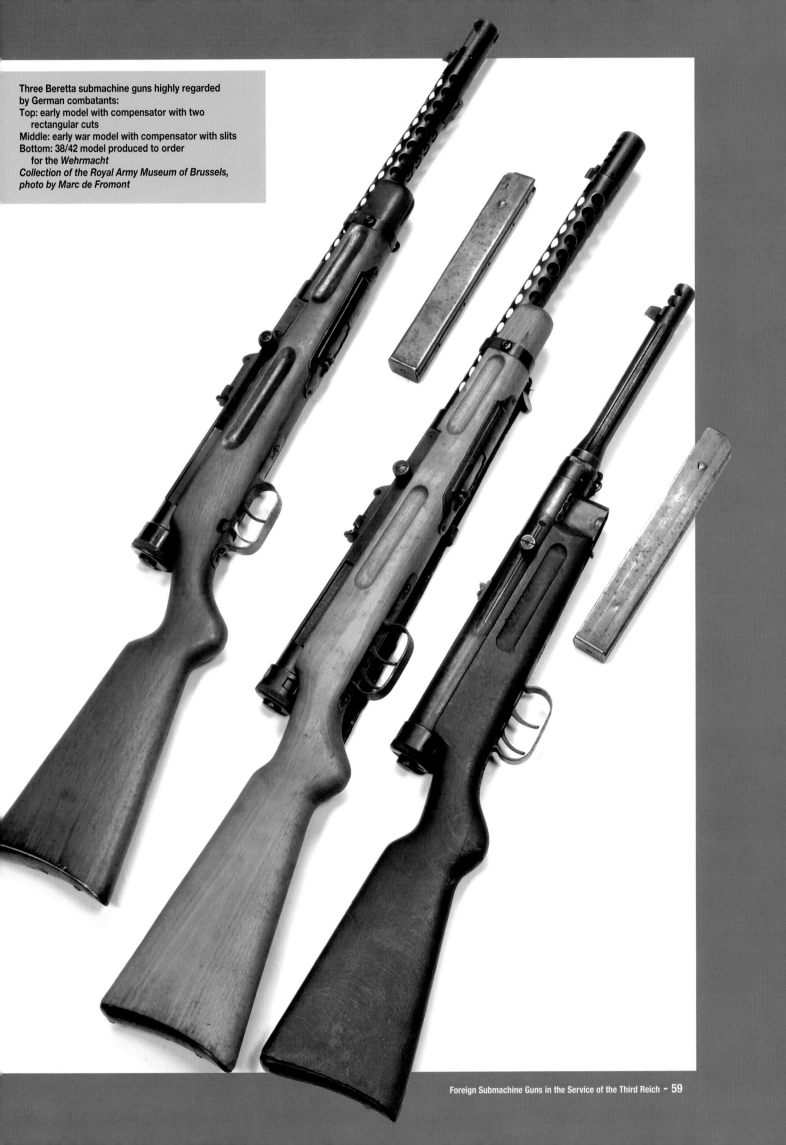

Three Beretta submachine guns highly regarded by German combatants:
Top: early model with compensator with two rectangular cuts
Middle: early war model with compensator with slits
Bottom: 38/42 model produced to order for the *Wehrmacht*
Collection of the Royal Army Museum of Brussels, photo by Marc de Fromont

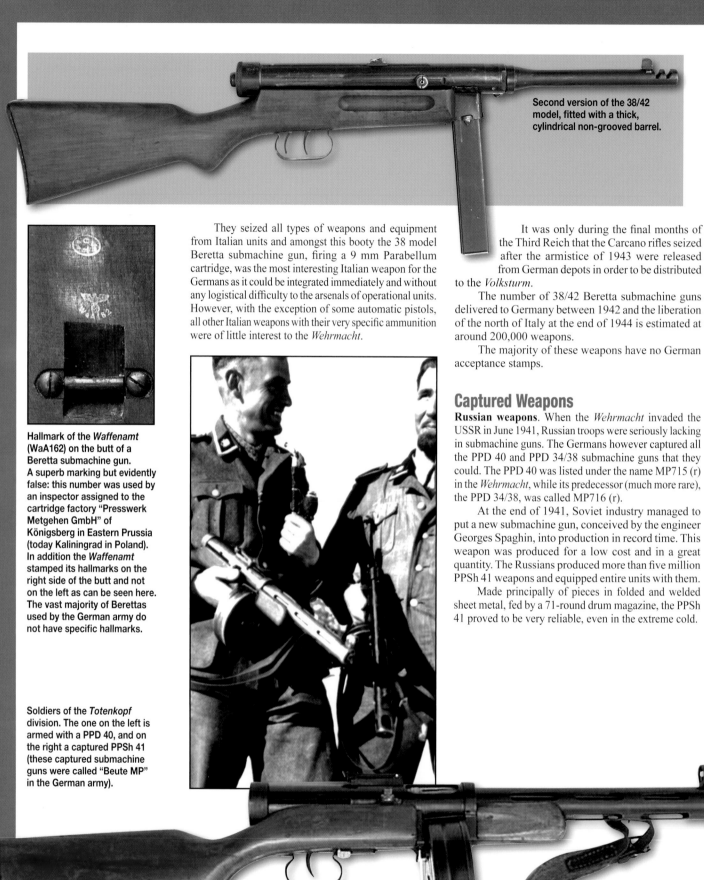

Second version of the 38/42 model, fitted with a thick, cylindrical non-grooved barrel.

Hallmark of the *Waffenamt* (WaA162) on the butt of a Beretta submachine gun. A superb marking but evidently false: this number was used by an inspector assigned to the cartridge factory "Presswerk Metgehen GmbH" of Königsberg in Eastern Prussia (today Kaliningrad in Poland). In addition the *Waffenamt* stamped its hallmarks on the right side of the butt and not on the left as can be seen here. The vast majority of Berettas used by the German army do not have specific hallmarks.

Soldiers of the *Totenkopf* division. The one on the left is armed with a PPD 40, and on the right a captured PPSh 41 (these captured submachine guns were called "Beute MP" in the German army).

They seized all types of weapons and equipment from Italian units and amongst this booty the 38 model Beretta submachine gun, firing a 9 mm Parabellum cartridge, was the most interesting Italian weapon for the Germans as it could be integrated immediately and without any logistical difficulty to the arsenals of operational units. However, with the exception of some automatic pistols, all other Italian weapons with their very specific ammunition were of little interest to the *Wehrmacht*.

It was only during the final months of the Third Reich that the Carcano rifles seized after the armistice of 1943 were released from German depots in order to be distributed to the *Volksturm*.

The number of 38/42 Beretta submachine guns delivered to Germany between 1942 and the liberation of the north of Italy at the end of 1944 is estimated at around 200,000 weapons.

The majority of these weapons have no German acceptance stamps.

Captured Weapons

Russian weapons. When the *Wehrmacht* invaded the USSR in June 1941, Russian troops were seriously lacking in submachine guns. The Germans however captured all the PPD 40 and PPD 34/38 submachine guns that they could. The PPD 40 was listed under the name MP715 (r) in the *Wehrmacht*, while its predecessor (much more rare), the PPD 34/38, was called MP716 (r).

At the end of 1941, Soviet industry managed to put a new submachine gun, conceived by the engineer Georges Spaghin, into production in record time. This weapon was produced for a low cost and in a great quantity. The Russians produced more than five million PPSh 41 weapons and equipped entire units with them.

Made principally of pieces in folded and welded sheet metal, fed by a 71-round drum magazine, the PPSh 41 proved to be very reliable, even in the extreme cold.

Modernized version of the PPD 34/38: the PPD was systematically recovered along with some very rare PPD 34/38s by soldiers of the *Wehrmacht* at the beginning of operation Barbarossa. This well-designed, good-quality weapon was abandoned by the Russians in favor of the Spaghin PPSh 41, as it was cheaper and quicker to produce.

This point is confirmed by a report of the September 13, 1942, signed by *SS-Obergruppenführer* Felix Steiner, a reputed soldier and commander of the SS *Wiking* division. In the report the superior reliability of the Russian weapon in cold climates and muddy terrain compared to their German equivalents is highlighted.

The Germans also appreciated the large-capacity magazine in the Russian submachine guns which gave its users a clear advantage in close quarter combat.

German soldiers therefore systematically recovered to their advantage the PPSh 41 captured during combat. The difference in caliber compared to German submachine guns posed very little problem as large quantities of 7.62 mm Tokarev ammunition used by the PPSh 41 had also been captured by the *Wehrmacht* from the Red Army.

The PPSh 41 was designated under the name MP717 (r) in the inventory of foreign weapons set up by the *Waffenamt*.

The return of units to Western Europe after a period on the Russian front led to the introduction of many PPSh 41 in western occupied countries and explains the presence of Russian weapons here.

Even after the end of the victorious advance in Russia, the Germans continued to recover many PPSh weapons. This was due to the tactic of the Red Army, relying essentially on frontal attacks, causing heavy losses of Russian soldiers and resulting in considerable equipment remaining in the field after the counter-offensives.

An attempt seems to have been made to convert the PPSh 9 mm caliber Parabellum by replacing the barrel and fitting the weapon with an adaptor allowing the use of MP40 magazines, but these tests were rapidly abandoned as they wasted a precious industrial potential.

If necessary, German cartridge factories were capable of supplying 7.63 mm Mauser cartridges used in the Russian army.

The use of an MP40 magazine meant the PPSh lost its most important quality: having a large capacity magazine which did not jam in the extreme cold.

Several Sudarev PPS 43 submachine guns were also used by the German army under the number (MP 719 (r), but their use was marginal compared to that of the PPSh 41.

This low use of the PPS 43 by the German army is doubtless explained by the fact that the PPS 43 was not widely distributed by the Red Army until after 1943, at the time when the period of defeat was beginning for the *Wehrmacht* and therefore when it recovered less equipment from the enemy.

Czech weapons. Before the Second World War, the Brno factory had developed an original submachine gun christened ZK 383. Like the Steyr Solothurn, this weapon was fitted with a recoil spring fitted in the butt, and its breech had a removable counterweight meaning the rate of fire could be modified at will.

Waffen-SS soldier armed with a ZK 383.

The ZK 383 was exported to Bulgaria and Venezuela.

When German troops entered Bohemia, the SS units, which at that time had virtually no modern weaponry, were allocated all available Czech weapons (ZB 37 machine guns, ZB 26 light machine guns, and VZ 24 carbines) for their use.

The few examples of the ZK 383 still stocked at Brno were also recovered by the SS but their numbers must have been greatly reduced as they only appear in photos of the period on the shoulder of soldiers of the "Black Order."

British weapons. From 1942, German forces had captured British Sten submachine guns during the failed landings carried out by the Anglo-Canadian forces at Dieppe.

A Sten seized at Dieppe was presented to the *Führer* who wrongly considered that if Great Britain was reduced to equipping its troops with such weapons then it meant that the country was most certainly at the end of the line!

Several months later, the Allies started to parachute the Sten in great number in occupied Europe, so as to enable the Resistance to act against the enemy.

Czech **ZK 383** submachine gun, several hundred of which were seized at Brno during the entry of German troops into Czechoslovakia. These weapons were most likely recovered by the *Waffen-SS*.

Russian PPSh 41 submachine gun. This weapon was made in very great quantities (around five million) by weapons factories in the eastern part of the USSR. It was very reliable in all weather conditions and particularly prized by German soldiers who often adopted it as a replacement for their supplied MP40, which was too often subject to jamming in the difficult conditions experienced in the Eastern front.

This corporal of the *Luftwaffe*, with an evident satisfaction, has just appropriated a brand new PPSh 41 from an equipment depot seized from the Red Army. As Russian 7.62 Tokarev ammunition had also been captured in great quantity during the first months of the war in the east, the supply for these weapons posed no problem.

Armenian soldiers of the *Wehrmacht* with a French flag in an occupied village. The officer on the left (arrow) is armed with a British Sten Mk.II submachine gun. *ECPA*

The number of Sten parachuted in France is estimated to be around 300,000 (essentially Mk.IIs). The Sten remains today the symbolic weapon of the resistance.

It is sometimes overlooked that a significant number of these parachute drops were intercepted by the enemy.

In the north of France, Belgium, and Holland several important resistance networks were broken up by the German security service and their radio operators were forced to broadcast under German control.

The Allies were leading a deception plan at that time with the objective of making the Germans believe that the landings would take place in the north of France and not in Normandy.

Even though the Allies knew that the radio operators of the dismantled networks broadcast under force, they continued the relationship with them by giving the German services false information concerning the site of the landings.

To round off this game of deception, they also broadcast the need to reinforce weapon supplies in the northern networks by intensifying parachute drops of equipment in that area, knowing perfectly well that they would, in reality, fall into the hands of the enemy.

Because of this trickery, the Allies were able to deceive the Germans concerning the real site of the landings and therefore to make sure that armored divisions were immobilized several hundred miles away from the Normandy coast.

For their part, the Germans "ordered" thousands of weapons and tons of various material and equipment under cover of false requests for supplies in the name of the resistance and which was parachuted to them by squadrons of the SOE (Special Operations Executive). This equipment was then collected on arrival by German security forces and transported to the Satory camp where it was stocked before another use was found for it.

Some of these weapons were subsequently transferred by the Reich Main Security Office (RSHA) to the French militia. Then in 1944, when the production of the MP40 had been stopped and the MP43 ammunition (which should have replaced that of the MP40) was not available in sufficient quantity, the *Wehrmacht* put into service the Sten captured by the RSHA as it was confronted by a great shortage of submachine guns.

The infamous Otto Skorzeny, head of the Friedenthal special unit had been seduced by the Sten.

Here is what he relates in his memoirs:

"I also learned at this Dutch Headquarters that we had excellent wireless communication with English stations. More than ten wireless sets, with all the codewords and keys, had been captured. By using these, and with the help of agents, we were able to hoodwink the English with a regular wireless communication with that country.

"From that moment, it was the enemy that takes responsibility of resolving our difficulties stoically. An inexpensive method that I highly recommend to all future commando leaders.

"The weapons parachuted into Holland, Belgium and France also included the British Sten gun. When I was examining it I was impressed by the simplicity of its construction and the fact that it was obviously cheap to produce. There must be a silencer for this weapon also, but Britain was keeping this refinement a secret – which was a compelling reason why I should get hold of one. This time however, the wireless request had no response. Either the British enemy smelt a rat, or the new weapon was being reserved for later use. I had, towards the end of June, the pleasure of being the first man in Germany to handle the silencer. I was most enthusiastic about the military possibilities of the weapon in its revised form. A reconnaissance party armed with it would avoid a lot of casualties! In the event of an unexpected meeting with the enemy, there would be no sound of firing to give it away.

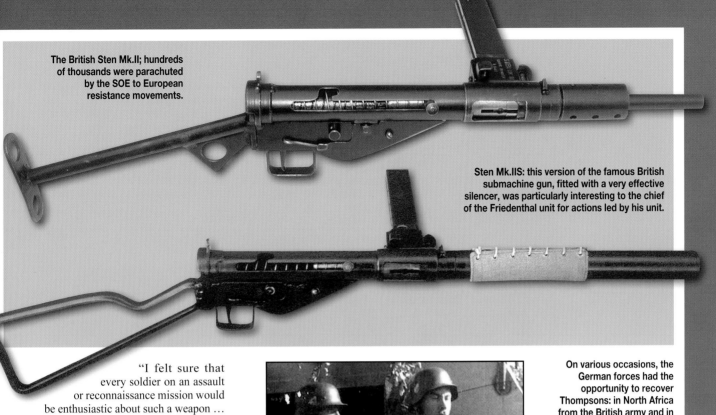

The British Sten Mk.II; hundreds of thousands were parachuted by the SOE to European resistance movements.

Sten Mk.IIS: this version of the famous British submachine gun, fitted with a very effective silencer, was particularly interesting to the chief of the Friedenthal unit for actions led by his unit.

"I felt sure that every soldier on an assault or reconnaissance mission would be enthusiastic about such a weapon … Apart from the silencer the Sten offered several advantages: it was far superior to the German submachine guns and for several reasons: much quicker to manufacture, it also cost significantly less than ours, which were however more accurate. The Sten could be dropped into the water, the snow, the dirt and it still worked. Not ours. Why not produce the silent Sten in quantity?

"I tried to convince two senior officers of the Military Economic and Armaments Office, whose commander was *General* Georg Thomas. I invited them to supper at Friedenthal: they were reluctant. It was spring, pleasant weather, so I suggested a walk in the park after supper. They agreed. We walked part of the way. Suddenly I stopped them.

"'Gentlemen,' I said to them, 'you are dead. And probably I too.'

"They collided in the darkness.

"'Dead? We're dead?'

"Behind us one of my people flashed his pocket lamp. He had the Sten with silencer in his hand and pointed at the empty shell casings on the ground. He had fired an entire magazine into the air. Our technicians of the armaments ministry were visibly very impressed by their theoretical and silent death. But the submachine gun lecture in the park achieved nothing. The answer I received from *General* Thomas' colleagues was:

"You are correct in principle. But, you admit yourself: the Sten submachine gun is no precision weapon. The Führer has repeatedly said that every German soldier has a right to the best weapons in every respect, and we could not accept responsibility for recommending the manufacture of a submachine gun that, even if silent, is less accurate than those already under production in Germany. *Heil Hitler*!'"

* Otto Skorzeny, *My Commando Operations*, Schiffer Publishing Ltd., 1995.

As we will see in the following chapter these first contacts with the Sten by the German forces had a profound influence on the production of essential weapons in the last months of the Third Reich.

On various occasions, the German forces had the opportunity to recover Thompsons: in North Africa from the British army and in France after the landings from Dieppe. We can see here soldiers on a German armored train with what seems to be a 1921 model Thompson possibly captured during the disarming of French units who were equipped with them after the invasion of the free zone.

SS-General Artur Phleps commander of the *Prinz Eugen* division, examines a British Sten Mk.2 taken from the enemy.

WEAPONS AT THE END OF THE WAR

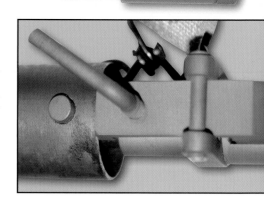

Copy of a Sten very close to the Gerät Potsdam but the maker is not identified. The silencer is to the right of the weapon. *Michel Moreau*

A Faithful Copy of the Sten Mk.II: the "Gerät Potsdam"

The defeats suffered on the eastern front, the destruction caused by the allied bombings and the success of the Normandy landings in June 1944 led to the more lucid elements of the supreme command of the *Wehrmacht* and the weapons ministry to envisage a possible invasion of Germany by the Russian forces in the east and the Anglo-American forces in the west.

The weapons and ammunition ministry therefore researched measures to continue supplying German combatants with weapons in a deteriorating industrial and military situation.

This was the "*Primitiv Waffen Programm*" which planned the manufacturing process of rifles, pistols, and rudimentary submachine guns in Germany during the last months of the war, weapons which today are designated by many collectors under the collective

Attachment of the silencer by bolting in a hole in the perforated case. *Michel Moreau*

"Gerät Potsdam": faithful copy of the British Sten Mk.II on a bench for the adjustment of the gun sights. *Mauser archive, via Walter Schmidt*

name "*Volksturm* Weapons." The will of the *Wehrmacht* high command to see the manufacture of a German version of the Sten, easy to produce in great quantity and at low cost, collided with the opposition of the *Führer*, who was also the supreme chief of the *Wehrmacht*.

The problem was eventually circumvented by the RSHA. Even though they were fanatically Nazi, the leaders of the RSHA were among the most well-informed in Germany concerning the course of the war. They were therefore under no illusions as to the outcome of military operations after June 1944.

In addition they thought coldly about the liberation of occupied territories and began setting up resistance movements that they hoped would be formed by the nationals of formerly occupied countries, sympathetic to the national-socialist ideology.

These resistance fighters would have as their mission to maintain a climate of agitation and instability in the zones newly liberated by the Allies.

In order to sustain confusion concerning their allegiance, it was decided that the men of these pro-German resistance groups would be equipped with the same type of weapons and equipment as those used by the Resistance organization during the German occupation before July 1944. The RSHA took up a project initiated by the *Abwehr* (which had just passed under its umbrella), and organized around 800 secret depots of weapons and equipment in occupied countries where parachuted agents could resupply.

The magazine housing, devoid of markings and the number 50 stamped on the weapon. *Michel Moreau*

In the following months, the advance of the Allied forces meant the Germans were gradually losing the source of supply of the Sten which was necessary for them to prepare the setting up of the resistance groups.

Due to the fact of not having enough captured Sten for this project, the RSHA took the initiative and placed an order for 25,000 copies of the Sten with the Mauser establishment at Oberndorf.

This manufacturing project was subject to the greatest secrecy. The copy of the Sten was christened under the code name of "Gerät Potsdam": "Potsdam Device."

Thomas B. Nelson highlights in his book *The World's Submachine Guns and Machine Pistols* that the operation was very costly as a credit of 1,800 Reichsmark was allocated to Mauser by the backers for every one of these Sten copies made by the Mauser company. This sum represented approximately ninety times the price of an authentic British Sten Mk.II!

The manufacture of the "Gerät Potsdam" was carried out in November and December 1944, at Mauser. Just under 10,000 (9,972 to be precise) were produced.

The majority of these weapons were hidden in hiding places organized by Reich secret service agents in Germany and in territories formerly occupied by the RSHA. Few of these hiding places were found; therefore the "Gerät Potsdam" is very rare today.

The museum of Oberndorf has today however an example of one of these "Gerät Potsdam," which is totally identical to a British Sten Mk.II. Only the method of making the magazine housing from a folded and welded outline on the under part the "Gerät Potsdam" from a British Sten.

A silencer, resembling a large tin can and sliding on the barrel, was also made for these weapons.

During the course of the in-depth research that he carried out on the Sten, Michel Moreau was able to examine an unusual example of a "Gerät Potsdam." This weapon, on the outside identical to a Sten Mk.II, had been made using traditional machining methods, meaning it is slightly heavier than the "real" Sten. In addition, on this example, the fire mode selector lever bears the initials "D" and "E" indicating the continuous burst and single shot fire capabilities in the German language, ("*Dauerfeuer*" and "*Einzelfeuer*"), instead of the letters A and S ("auto" and "single"), appearing on the fire mode selector lever on British-made weapons. Additionally, the magazine housing is immobilized by welding and does not accept Sten magazines but does accept those of the MP28. This second version of the "Gerät Potsdam" bears a "50" serial number and a miniscule naval anchor stamped on the skeleton butt. Mauser only produced a part of this order made by the RSHA, and it is legitimate to wonder if the remainder of this order was entrusted to another manufacturer.

German marking on the fire mode selector. *Michel Moreau*

The two folded sides forming the magazine housing are assembled by solid welding. *Mauser archive, via Walter Schmidt*

Members of the *Volksturm* assembled in Berlin to listen to a speech by Dr. Joseph Goebbels. An MG3 and several carbines can be seen, but the *Panzerfaust* (individual antitank weapon) is by far the most common weapon and, in this respect, this rocket launcher is emblematic of the desperate resistance in Germany. In the guerilla fighting and street combat that the *Volksturm* organizers predicted, the use of basic submachine guns made sense.

The Poor Man's Sten: the "Gerät Neumünster" or MP3008

Marking on a butt resembling a small naval anchor.
Michel Moreau

The silencer.
Michel Moreau

The technical services of the *Wehrmacht*, more objective than their *Führer*, considered that the Sten was a perfect response to the urgency of the situation in the last months of 1944.

Albert Speer, weapons and ammunitions minister, shared this view and was favorable to the emergency production of simplified weapons (*Primitiv Waffen*).

The *Wehrmacht*, informed of the existence of the "Gerät Potsdam" project, requested Mauser to conceive a simplified version where the manufacture could be spread between small enterprises thereby more likely to avoid Allied aerial bombings.

To answer this request, one of the most talented creators of the Mauser firm, Ludwig Vorgrimler, designed a weapon inspired by the Sten, but without a perforated barrel case. On this weapon, the barrel is immobilized in the receiver before being permanently welded there. The receiver itself was formed from a rolled leaf of metal, welded at the front and rear. The non-welded central part constituted the groove in which the bolt handle slid.

The magazine housing was no longer horizontal and mobile as on the Sten but vertical and welded in position.

The work time necessary to make this submachine gun was estimated at one hour. The weapon was fed by MP40 magazines. The first submachine guns of this type were fitted with a butt in flat wood, then with a "T" shaped butt, copied from the No.2 butt on the Sten but where the grip does not have a circular cut that is a feature on English-made weapons.

Subsequently these weapons were mounted with "skeleton" butts quite similar to the No.3 butt mounted on some British Stens.

This second project, aiming to develop a simplified version of the Sten was christened "Gerät Neumünster."

In the listings of the *Waffenamt*, the weapon received the reference number (*Gerät Nummer*): "1-3-3008" and post-war was called "MP 3008."

Nevertheless, as W. Darrin Weaver mentions in his work dedicated to weapons of the *Volksturm* (*Desperate Measures*), this submachine gun was simply called "*Volksmaschinenpistole*" ("Submachine gun of the people") by official Nazi authorities and quite simply "*Sten Maschinenpistole*" by its users.

It seems that Mauser initially made two specimens of the Gerät Neumünster, which were presented to the German technical services, who tested them and gave a favorable opinion concerning their mass production, after requesting a few detailed modifications. Once given the green light, Mauser made a small series of around 150, designed to serve as models of reference for the factories involved in the manufacture program of this "*Volksmaschinenpistole*."

Weaver determined that there were fourteen assembly centers receiving components made by thirty factories working as sub-contractors.

These two "*Volksmaschinenpistolen*" MP3008 with a large model *Panzerfaust* 30, a *Volksturm* armband, and a P.38 pistol symbolize the desperate combats led in 1945 by the German population. Note that the MP3008 at the bottom is fitted with a bolt handle crossing the receiver as on the Mk.5 adopted on the Sten at the end of the war. The MP3008 at the top has a receiver rolled and welded at the rear and front of the cocking slot as well as at the front of the ejection port. *Collection of the Royal Army Museum of Brussels, photo by Marc de Fromont*

DEUTSCHER VOLKSSTURM
WEHRMACHT

These multiple manufacturing sites explain the slight differences in detail that can be seen between the various MP3008 today.

The MP3008 resulted initially from an order from the German army (*Heer*), destined to arm the regular troops and not an order from the national socialist party, with the aim of arming the *Volksturm*, contrary to what a great many collectors thought before the publication of Weaver's book.

Once the production for the army was begun, another order for these weapons was placed by the Nazi government for the *Volksturm*.

Among the weapons leaving the same factory at the same time, there were some which were stamped with the manufacturer's code, the initial "H" of the land army and which bore an inspection mark of the *Waffenamt*, whereas others had no markings other than a number. The current hypothesis is that the first were destined for the regular *Wehrmacht* troops and the second for the *Volksturm*.

Various other companies took part in the manufacture of the MP3008 or some of its parts but their list remains very difficult to establish today with certainty as many archives of that period were destroyed or lost. Researchers who study this weapon are also obstructed by the fact that some codes remain as yet unknown.

The assemblers of the MP3008 are today identified as follows:

- C.G. Haenel Waffen und Faradisation (code "fxo")

- ERMA, it would seem components for the MP3008 but not complete weapons

- W.J. Hôlzen (code not identified)

- Gottfried Linder A.G. (code "dxl")

- Gustav Appel: company in Spandau, well known for its RG 34 cleaning kits that it supplied in great quantity to the *Wehrmacht* throughout the entire war (code "cnx")

- Gerhard & Schubert of Amberg (code "DCO")

- Gerhard Glos & Voll of Würtzburg, (code not identified)

- Walther Steiner of Stuhl (code "nea")

- Blohm & Voss. The submachine guns made by the great naval shipyard in Hamburg had a different appearance from the other MP3008: the rear of the barrel is surrounded by a perforated cooling jacket. They are

also fitted with either a flat butt in wood or a "T" shaped butt, with a pistol grip. These weapons are marked with the initials "B" and "V" of the firm in two circles.

- Karl Eickhorn. This cutlery manufacturer of Solingen, with close links to the Nazi party, seems to have produced only 26 MP3008 (code "RDE") before the arrival of the Allies (code "cof" and perhaps "RDE" at the end of the war).

In addition, other non-identified codes such as "tjg," "tvw," or "TJK" have been seen on some MP3008 without their manufacturer being as yet identified.

The only accessory supplied with the MP3008 was a canvas sling, generally made of a gas mask box strap.

In his book on German rifle grenades and grenade throwers (*Deutsche Gewehrgranaten und Gewehrgranatengeräte bis 1945*), German historian Michael Heidler points out the services of the *Waffenamt* tried an MP3008 fitted with a grenade thrower case at the Kummersdorf firing range on January 11, 1945. The 9 mm Parabellum (Treibpatrone 08) propelling cartridge

MP 3008 produced by the Blohm & Voss naval shipyard.

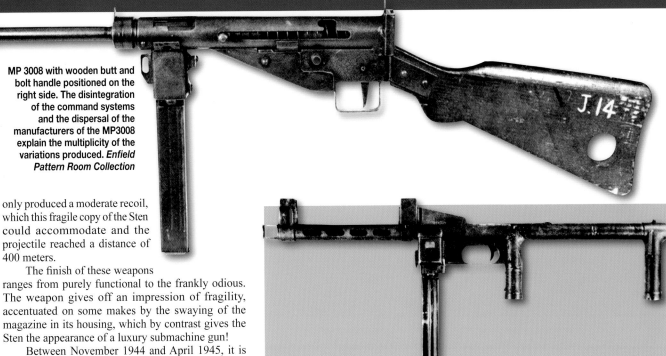

only produced a moderate recoil, which this fragile copy of the Sten could accommodate and the projectile reached a distance of 400 meters.

The finish of these weapons ranges from purely functional to the frankly odious. The weapon gives off an impression of fragility, accentuated on some makes by the swaying of the magazine in its housing, which by contrast gives the Sten the appearance of a luxury submachine gun!

Between November 1944 and April 1945, it is estimated that 3,000 to 5,000 submachine guns were made in the territory of the Reich.

Just like the "Gerät Potsdam," the MP3008 weapons seem to have mysteriously disappeared. Few weapons of this type have been found, others were buried in hiding places managed by the resistance movements (*Wehrwolf*) that the Nazi party hoped to see develop in areas conquered by the Allies, or destroyed by bombing or perhaps even destroyed by the manufacturers before the arrival of the Allies.

The Volksmaschinenpistole Erma EMP 44

This mysterious weapon resembles a "primitive weapon" in the same vein as the MP3008. However, the specimen number 00015, still in the museum of the US Army in Aberdeen, Maryland, today, bears a marking indicating that it was made by ERMA in February 1943.

The Volksmaschinenpistole Erma (EMP 44).

More a result of bad plumbing rather than expert weaponry, it bears a wider magazine housing in which it is possible to position two MP40 magazines side by side in a transporter fairly similar to that found on the MP40/1.

Even though its basic appearance means it is presented in the chapter dedicated to weapons of the end of the war, the date of manufacture of the EMP 44 conserved in Aberdeen seems too early for a weapon of the "*Primitiv Waffen Programm*."

In addition, the double magazine system, that unnecessarily complicated the manufacture of this model, seems incongruous on a weapon of the last months of the war.

It is possible that the EMP 44 is simply an unfinished prototype of a close quarter defense weapon, designed to be mounted on tanks or fortifications to cover blind spots.

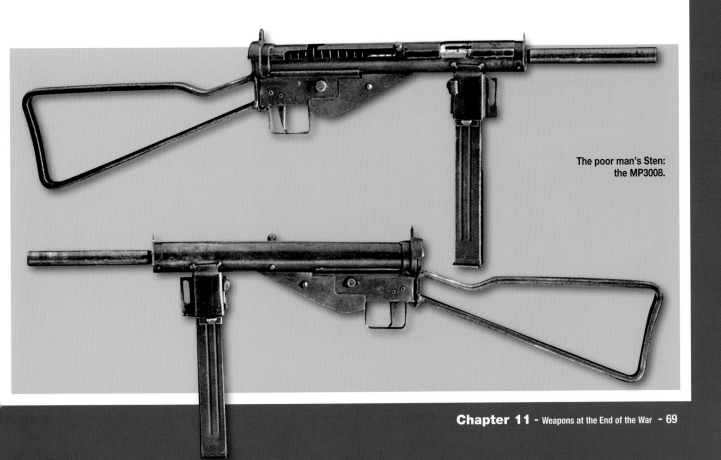

The poor man's Sten: the MP3008.

CHAPTER 12

ASSAULT RIFLES MKb 42, MP43/1, MP44, AND STG44

The Haenel 42 model Maschinenkarabiner [MKb 42(H)], a promising weapon chambered for the 7.92 mm Kurtz cartridge. *Hermann Historica*

American soldier examining some brand new MKb 42 (W) weapons at the Walther factories in Zella Mehlis. *US Army*

Marking on the receiver of the MKb 42 (H). The bolt handle blocked in the safety groove, seen here, constitutes the only safety mechanism of the weapon, which bears no safety catch.

The base of the backsight on the MKb 42 and the MP43/1 has two ribs used to fix the special mount for the ZF 41 sight; As this sight was not satisfactory, the ribs did not feature on subsequent models.

with their rifle or carbine above that distance. The powerful 7.92 x 57 mm cartridge fired by German shoulder arms came into its own when it was used in a submachine gun or a rifle with a sight.

Several weapons firing ammunition of an intermediate length, between the 9 mm pistol cartridge and the 7.92 mm rifle cartridge were studied by several inventors and proposed to the *Reichswehr* between the wars.

In an effort to standardize ammunition, the *Reichswehr* refrained from adopting intermediate ammunition and kept two cartridges:

- 7.92 x 57 mm for rifles and machine guns

- 9 mm Parabellum for pistols and submachine guns

The *Reichswehr* however continued to secretly but actively support research into semi-automatic carbines with high capacity magazines and selective firing during the wars.

S ome readers may be surprised to see assault rifles presented in a special issue dedicated to German submachine guns. We are dedicating a chapter however to these weapons as the majority of models bear the name "*Maschinenpistole*" and because it was planned they would replace the carbine K.98k and the MP40 submachine gun within the combat groups of the *Wehrmacht*.

Development of an "Intermediary" Cartridge

From the end of the First World War, the German army admitted that the rifle and carbine cartridge was unnecessarily powerful for normal combat distances (less than 400 meters in general) and that few men in reality were capable of carrying out effective shots

MKb 42 (W): a good-looking weapon whose complexity of manufacture and sensitivity to dirt meant it was abandoned by the *Waffenamt. Enfield Pattern Room Collection*

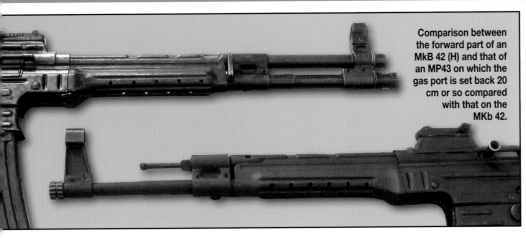

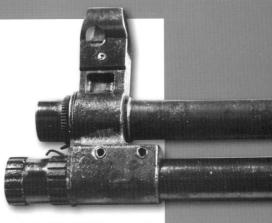

Comparison between the forward part of an MkB 42 (H) and that of an MP43 on which the gas port is set back 20 cm or so compared with that on the MKb 42.

On the MKb 42(H) the gas port is positioned at the end of the barrel.

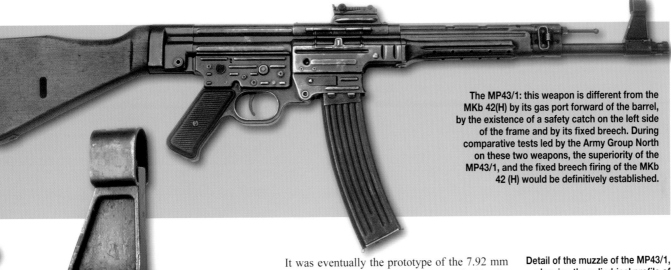

The MP43/1: this weapon is different from the MKb 42(H) by its gas port forward of the barrel, by the existence of a safety catch on the left side of the frame and by its fixed breech. During comparative tests led by the Army Group North on these two weapons, the superiority of the MP43/1, and the fixed breech firing of the MKb 42 (H) would be definitively established.

It was eventually the prototype of the 7.92 mm caliber cartridge with a 33 mm case, researched by the Polte cartridge factory of Magdebourg, which was taken on by the *Wehrmacht* in 1941. All that remained was to develop the weapon that was to fire it!

Towards a New Type of Shoulder Weapon

Along with the majority of prototypes of that time, the MKb 35 Vollmer was excellent but unfortunately too complex to be manufactured on a large scale. When Germany started its rearmament in 1934, the need for equipment was such that the industrialists had to concentrate on the production of the two basic weapons of the infantry: the MG34 machine gun and the K.98k carbine. From 1938, the MP38 submachine gun was added to the list of weapons to be produced as an absolute priority. Consequently, the project for weapons with intermediate ammunition was left in abeyance for several years.

Such a weapon only comes into its own when using an intermediary cartridge, the *Reichswehr* encouraged therefore some industrialists to carry out research in that domain. That is how BKIW (formerly DWM) and Rheinmetall came to develop highly promising ammunition, with a lighter bullet than that of a rifle and a shorter cartridge case (between 33 and 46 mm). The engineer Heinrich Vollmer, in association with the firm GECO, studied a cartridge with a 35 mm case designed to be fired in a semi-automatic carbine of his conception: the MKb 35.

Detail of the muzzle of the MP43/1, showing the cylindrical profile of the barrel, the wide foresight base and the long protective cover of the muzzle threads.

Detail view showing:
- the marking MP43/1,
- the serial number followed by an oblique bar and the two last digits of the year of manufacture (43 for 1943)
- the marking awt of the WMF (A) company (Würtembergiche Metawarenfabrik), which produced the grip blocks of the MP43/1 and MP43 as a sub-contractor
- the safety catch (B)
- the fire mode selector (C)

Note on this early production weapon that the magazine catch is still crisscrossed on its entire surface

Detail of the MP43 receiver serial number 7180 c made in 1943. On this early production MP43, the code awt of the WTF company is on the grip block. The base of the backsight has no fixation ribs for a sight, which existed on the MKb 42 and the MP43/1.

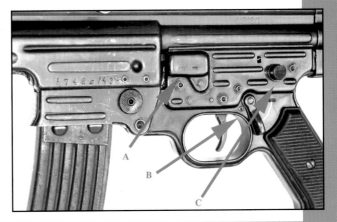

MP44 cartridges were delivered on clips of five and in boxes of fifteen or twenty.

MP44 used for training: the cut makes the gas vent hole visible.

Another view of a training MP44 shows the ingenious principle of manufacturing the weapon. The half shells which shape the receiver encircle a machined block of steel (painted in red) in which the barrel is housed.
Jean-François Legendre

The mobilization of 1939 added a new element to the problem by depriving German weapons' factories of a large part of their specialized labor. As much for reasons of preserving army numbers as for reasons of principle, it was impossible to withdraw highly specialized workers en masse from the front in order to assign them to the "domestic front," (clearly to return them to the weapons factories where they had worked, with a status of "special appointment").

After the beginning of operations in Russia and North Africa, the *Wehrmacht* was confronted with a heightened need for weapons. Foreign voluntary personnel, replacing German mobilized workers, did not generally possess the same degree of professional training and were in any event not impassioned by a rock solid faith in the Third Reich.

Experts from the ministry of armaments were therefore encouraged to conduct research in all domains; production methods which could be ensured by low-skilled labor and without any particular patriotic motivation and which could be shared over dispersed production units so as to be less vulnerable to bombing raids.

Mountain troops belonging to the Army Group North, equipped with MP43/1 used for comparative tests with the MKb 42 (H) carried out on the eastern front in April 1943. Note that the soldier has camouflaged his weapon by painting it white. *ECPA*

For infantry weapons which had to be made in large quantities, it meant adopting models with the absolute minimum of machined parts (barrel, actuator, and breech). Other parts were made from pressing sheets of steel and then welding; the very high level of mastery acquired by German metal workers in pressing metal meant that several manufacturers were able to propose some interesting models: Walther & Haenel proposed a weapon called Machinenkarabiner 42 (Machinenkarabiner = automatic carbine or MKb for short).

The two prototypes were named MKb 42(W) for the prototype Walther and MKb42 (H) for Haenel. These short and compact weapons, fitted with a 30-round magazine and having a selective fire capacity, fired the intermediate 7.92 x 33 mm cartridge, developed by Plote, which would go on to take the name of model 43 cartridge and also "7.9 Kurtz."

The weapon proposed by Walter bore a ring shaped piston surrounding the barrel and was vulnerable to dirt. Its realization demanded very precise machining but did not answer the demands of the moment; the development of the MKb 42(W) was therefore abandoned.

The MKb 42 (H), a weapon in 7.92 x 33 mm caliber, firing with open breech, and fitted with a fire selector giving the user a choice between single shot or continuous burst fire, had been conceived by Hugo Schmeisser. This weapon, made by Haenel in association with a firm specializing in the manufacture of pressed metal parts: Merz Werke (code "cos"), seemed to answer the needs of the *Wehrmacht*.

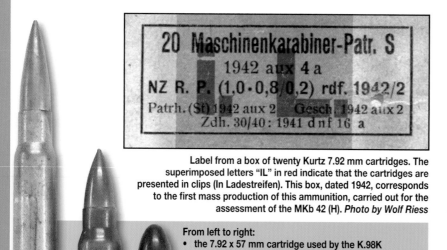

20 Maschinenkarabiner-Patr. S
1942 aux 4 a
NZ R. P. (1,0·0,8/0,2) rdf. 1942/2
Patrh. (St) 1942 aux 2   Gesch. 1942 aux 2
Zdh. 30/40 : 1941 dnf 16 a

Label from a box of twenty Kurtz 7.92 mm cartridges. The superimposed letters "IL" in red indicate that the cartridges are presented in clips (In Ladestreifen). This box, dated 1942, corresponds to the first mass production of this ammunition, carried out for the assessment of the MKb 42 (H). *Photo by Wolf Riess*

From left to right:
- the 7.92 x 57 mm cartridge used by the K.98K carbine, the G.42, and G.43 semi-automatic rifles, the FG42 parachutist rifle and the MG34 and MG42 machine guns.
- the 7.92 x 33 mm "intermediate" cartridge (also called 7.92 Kurtz or Patrone M.43 of the MKb 42, MP/43, 44, and StG44 assault rifles,
- the 9 x 9 mm cartridge (also called 9 mm Parabellum or Patron 08) of the MP40 and P.38 and P.08 pistols.

From top to bottom: MP43/1, MP44, and StG44
showing various types of butts, grip plates, and finishes.
Collection of the Royal Army Museum of Brussels,
photo by Marc de Fromont

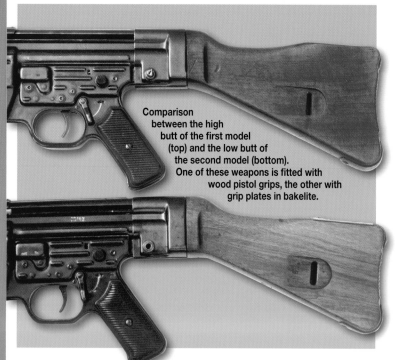

Comparison between the high butt of the first model (top) and the low butt of the second model (bottom). One of these weapons is fitted with wood pistol grips, the other with grip plates in bakelite.

15 Pistolenpatronen 43 m. E.
1944 wa 18
Nz. R. P. (1,0-0,8/0,2): 1944 rdf. 11 - 1,57 g
Para. (St) — 1944 wa
Gesch. — 1944 kam
Zdh. 30/40 — 1944 emp 285

Rare label on a box of 200 model 43 cartridges made in 1942. *Photo by Wolf Riess*

14 Pistolenpatronen 43 m. E.
1944 wa 6
Nz. R. P. (1,0-0,8/0,2): 1944 rdf. 3 — 1,58 g
Patrh. (St) — 1944 wa   Gesch. — 1944 wa
Zdh. 30/40 — 1944 faa 129

Surprising box of 14 cartridges doubtless conceived to fill 28-round magazines. *Photo by Wolf Riess*

Marking on an MP44 receiver. The grip block has been supplied by the Fritz Werner AG company of Berlin, indicated by the *Waffenamt WaA29* control stamp.

This StG44 shows a finish typical of the end of the war characterized by a mix of bronzed parts (the very dark aspect of the bronzing is due to the lack of finish of the surfaces), parkerized parts or those treated with phosphoric acid, as on the grip shown here. *Collection of the Royal Army Museum of Brussels, photo by Marc de Fromont*

The Veto of the *Führer*

However, when the MKb42 (H) was presented to Adolf Hitler on April 14, 1942, the *Führer* opposed a total veto of the continuation of research of this model. He contented himself with authorizing that weapons undergoing assembly were completed.

A veteran of the Great War, Hitler remained a fervent defender of the traditional rifle cartridge and wanted the efforts of the weapons engineers to concentrate on the development of automatic rifles firing 7.92 x 57mm cartridges such as the G.41 and 43, the prototype of the assault rifle researched by Gustloff-Werke, as well as the FG42 parachutist rifle.

The supreme commander of the German army was very concerned that German soldiers should have equipment superior to that of the enemy constantly at their disposal. By putting in service the "7.92 Kurtz" caliber weapons, he feared that German troops equipped with it would find themselves in a position of inferiority when faced with an enemy using traditional infantry cartridges with a greater range.

The decision of the *Führer* hindered the enthusiasm of the creators of the MKb 42 (H) and caused great delays in the weapon development program. However, this edict never totally interrupted the process of research.

Strengthened by the authorization given by Hitler to finish the assembly of the MKb 42 (H) that were being made, the creators of the weapon used the ambiguity of this order to pursue the improvement of their weapon.

Courageously disobedient, several senior members of the general staff discreetly ordered that the tests already started be completed.

Several dozen MKb 42 (H) were entrusted to the infantry school at Döbertitz, which confirmed the interest in the weapon while recommending several minor ergonomic modifications (repositioning of the sling swivels, shortening of the magazine, addition of a hand guard, removal of the guideway for reloading the magazine, etc.).

In parallel, the technicians at Haenel were hampering away at their research in order to respond to a criticism of the *Wehrmacht*, who did not like the fact that the MKb 42 fired with open breech.

In November 1942, Haenel was in a position to propose an MKb 42 version firing with closed breech and fitted with an internal percussion hammer, as well as a safety catch positioned on the left side of the frame. This type of firing gave the weapon a much greater stability during continuous burst fire and a greater precision during single shot fire.

The weapon thus modified was therefore able to replace both the MP40 and the K.98 carbine in usual combat distances.

The stability during continuous burst fire was further improved by moving back the gas port from the muzzle at a third of the barrel length and adopting a more ergonomic grip and butt.

During the process, Haenel took the opportunity of abandoning the bayonet stud which had initially been on the MKb 42 (H) to satisfy the more traditional elements in the army. This improved version was called MP43/1, the choice of the initials MP (*Maschinenpistole*) was designed to hide the fact that research forbidden by the Führer was in fact being pursued by making it appear that it concerned work carried out on a new submachine gun and not on a carbine!

MP 44 made in 1944: apart from the name, nothing distinguishes this weapon from the MP43.

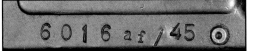

The considerable increase in production of the StG44 in the last months of the war led to the use of double letters in front of the number, even though these makes were gradually stopped between January and April 1945, as the zones in which the factories making them progressively fell into the hands of the Allies. *Collection of the Royal Army Museum of Brussels, photo by Marc de Fromont*

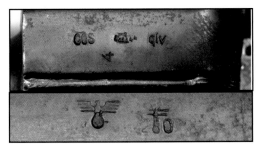

The qlv marking is the code of the ERMA factory of Erfurt and the "Eagle 280" control stamp is that assigned to the ERMA factory by the *Waffenamt* and stamped on finished sets. This example has been assembled from elements supplied by the sub-contractor Merz-Werke as the code "cos" and the stamp WaA44 can be seen. According to information supplied by Hugo Schmeisser, ERMA was the second producer of MP44 weapons with 104,000 delivered.

Comparative tests were carried out on the Russian front between the MKb 42 (H), christened for the occasion the MP43 A, and the MP43/1 which was designated the name of MP43 B for the period of testing.

The version B, in other words the MP43/1, clearly outclassed the version A.

The enthusiastic reports from the *Gebirgsjäger*, who had been supplied with the MP43/ 1 for experimental purposes, won over the high command, who then applied themselves to convincing Hitler of the merits of adopting this new weapon, which would bring a greatly superior fire power to the German soldier compared to that of a rifle or a submachine gun. In addition it would not impose excess weight and so cause reduced mobility as machine guns would have done.

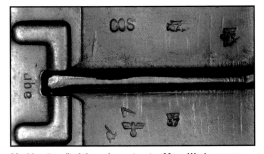

Marking "cos" of the sub-contractor Merz-Werke on an MP44 made by Haenel as indicated by the "eagle/37" stamp. According to statements made by Hugo Schmeisser after the war, Haenel was the the principle manufacturer of assault rifles with 185,000 examples of the MP43, MP44, and StG44 made.

Gerbirgsjäger of Army Group North firing an MP43/1. Interestingly, this man has a *Luftwaffe* aircrew knife on his belt. This photo illustrates the necessity of wearing thick gloves during frigid operations with a weapon having maximum metal parts. *ECPA*

A demonstration was organized the February 6, 1943, for the benefit of the *Führer* who nonetheless maintained his veto, the general inspector of the infantry courageously planned some new tests in troop units which consisted of giving combatants of Army Group North, fighting on the Russian front, 1,500 MKb 42s, which were soon to be replaced by several thousand MP43/1s. The command of the Northern army groups totally played along and withdrew the MP40 and K.98k from service in the battalions that were fully equipped with the new weapon. Only the MG34 and MG42 machine guns and the K.98k with sights were kept as old equipment.

Hitler Accepts the MP43/1

The German elements equipped with the MP43/1 for experimental purposes were able to defeat the Russian troops even though the Germans were very greatly outnumbered. The reports of these actions finally carried the decision. The *Führer* accepted this new weapon, which became even more urgent as the Red Army was receiving en masse PPSh 41 submachine guns, which meant it could equip entire divisions with automatic weapons.

The MP43/1 started large scale manufacture at Haenel from components supplied by many various sub-contractors including Merz-Werke.

On October 1, 1943, after a meeting with the head of the technical department of the weapons and ammunitions division of the ministry of armaments, Hitler finally acquiesced to the cause of the MP43 and ordered the total stoppage of the manufacture of the MP40 in favor of the MP43. This decision was slightly premature as, disrupted by Allied bombing and starting to lack raw materials, German industry was experiencing great difficulty in supplying the MP43 requested along with the 7.92 Kurtz ammunition. It was estimated that every assault rifle fired 6,000 shots per month.

StG44 marking for "*Sturmgewehr*" meaning "assault rifle," this name replaced that of the MP44 in November 1944. Without being aware of it, the senior civil servants of the Reich propaganda ministry had created a name which would go on to be translated in several languages and still remains in use today. *Collection of the Royal Army Museum of Brussels, photo by Marc de Fromont*

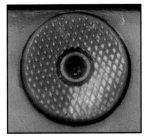

Magazine bolt lever with grid pattern on an MP43/1.

Lever with concentric circles on a StG44.

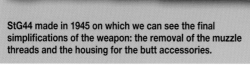

StG44 made in 1945 on which we can see the final simplifications of the weapon: the removal of the muzzle threads and the housing for the butt accessories.

Marking "byf" of the Mauser factory which produced several elements of the Sturmgewehr: essentially these were grips, bases for the butt and also several elements of the receiver which were mounted by Haenel and whose "Eagle 37" stamp can be seen at the bottom.

A badly-stamped "bnz" bears witness to the slackness which reigned at the end of the war. Steyr was in third position in the ranking of 7.92 Ku assault rifle manufacturers with 88,000 made.

Marking "qlv" on a transporter made by ERMA.

"Eagle/280" stamp on the glued laminated butt of an ERMA-made MP44.

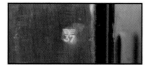

"Eagle 37" stamp on a Haenel made magazine.

Code "jvd" on this butt reinforcement made by the Czech factory Este Nordbömiche Metallwarenfabrik. This code is sometimes found on certain parts of a P.38.

The OKW (*Oberkomman-do der Wehrmacht*) or the supreme command of the German armed forces wished, for its part, to totally replace the K.98k/MP40 duo with the MP43.

The general staff began by making the adoption of the new weapon official on March 16, 1944, under the name MP44.

With a view to transforming the MP44 into a universal weapon, tests were made to use the MP44 as a sniper rifle. The infantry school at Döberitz tested the MP44 equipped with a guide way welded on the right side of the receiver, on which the base of a ZF4 sight was fixed. The MP44 with sight and ammunition proved nonetheless to be incapable of replacing the K.98k with sight used over long distances by snipers.

At the end of the war, the German army leaned towards the generalization of the MP43 firing the 7.92 Kurtz, the almost total abandonment of the MP40 and keeping the rifles with sight (K.98k, G.41, and G.43) as well as the MG 42 machine gun in 7.92 x 57 mm caliber. This conception would later influence the Red Army who during the Cold War would equip all its men with Kalashnikov assault rifles while simultaneously keeping two weapons in its combat groups chambered for long cartridges: the SVD Dragunov sniper rifle and the PK light machine gun.

Developments and Variations

According to statements made to the Allies by Hugo Schmeisser just after the war, a total of 420,000 MP43, MP44, and StG44 assault rifles were made principally by four manufacturers:

- Haenel
- ERMA
- Steyr-Daimler-Puch
- Sauer & Sohn

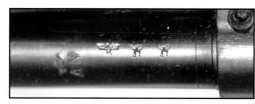

Stamp on a Haenel-made barrel.

Marking on a barrel made by Steyr-Daimler-Puch A.G.

Code "ayf" on the barrel of an MP44 made by ERMA.

Code "ar" of the Berlin subsidiary of Mauser (Mauser-Borsigwalde) on the breech of an MP44.

The initials in gothic cursive script on an element of the receiver supplied by Sauer & Sohn to Haenel, where the "eagle 37" stamp identifies the final assembler. At the end of the war, Sauer & Sohn ensured the assembly of complete weapons from subcontracted parts. Its production is estimated at 55,000 according to statements made to the Allies by Hugo Schmeisser. The hand guard bears the code "aqr" allocated to the R&O Lux Metallwaren-u.Maschinenfabrik company.

Around 12,000 MKb 42(H) and 14,000 MP43/1, which continued to be used until the end of the war in addition to the MP43, MP44, and StG44 should be added to these weapons.

The weapon was subsequently subject to many changes of name as well as changes in detail:

- The cylindrical barrel was replaced by a barrel in tiered sections. The smaller diameter section of barrel being at the front, along with the adoption of a new sight base, smaller than on the MP43/1, meant the standard grenade sleeve for the K.98k carbine could be mounted. Whereas the MP43/1 had to use a specific grenade sleeve which screwed on to the muzzle of the barrel. This version with a tiered barrel was called MP43 and was produced in 1943 and 1944.

- Originally the MP43/1 had been conceived to be used with the small ZF 41 sight with a magnification of 1.5 mounted on some K.98k. To this end the sight base on the first MP43/1 weapons bears ribs on both sides on which a special base can be mounted. The right rib has a locking notch allowing the sight support to be immobilized. This notch disappeared on the late production MP43/1 models (which translated to the ZF 41 option being abandoned by the manufacturer).

An MP44 with accessories evoking the last days of the Third Reich: 1943 model stick grenade (an example with a chipped handle), an antipersonnel mine, *Panzerfaust 30 "Klein,"* and a crate with two drum magazines for a cartridge belt. *Collection of the Royal Army Museum of Brussels, photo by Marc de Fromont*

In the foreground a standard butt with a brace and a flap giving access to the housing for accessories. In the background a simplified butt mounted on a StG44 made in 1945, made of a single piece of pine and having no housing for accessories.

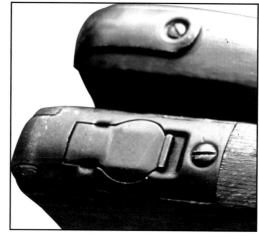

First model breech on the left and second model on the right. The oblique groove (arrow) added to the second model meant the residue left after firing, (this residue came from the protective laquer on the bullet casing), had a place to go without it obstructing the repetitive movements of firing.

- Then the ribs on both sides of the sight base, having become unnecessary, were removed from the MP43 and subsequent models.

- Several parts of the mechanism were subject to minor modifications which improved the use of the weapon, reinforced its reliability or made it easier to manufacture.
- adoption of a lower butt to make shouldering the weapon easier.

- piercing of a hole in the cube shaped block housing the piling pin forward of the gas cylinder. The disassembly rod positioned in the butt housing could be introduced in this hole to facilitate the unscrewing of this part.

- filing of a transversal groove above the breech. Firing residue (in particular residues of lacquer used to protect the cartridge cases) and foreign bodies entering the mechanism could become lodged in this groove rather than blocking the movement of the breech.

- increase of the number of orifices of the hand guard, probably to improve the cooling of the barrel.

- withdrawal of the butt plates made from bakelite on certain models in favor of a version in wood in order to economize on the components which went in to the manufacture of bakelite.

On the March 16, 1944, the general staff of the *Wehrmacht*, anxious to end the confusion concerning the names, renamed the MP44 weapon without it being subject to any mechanical change during its manufacture.

In November 1944, it was once again decided to change the name of the weapon which became *Sturmgewehr* (assault rifle) 44 (StG44 for short). This change of name was for propaganda purposes. In the desperate situation that Germany found itself in at that time, the propaganda ministry was still trying to maintain combativeness in giving the weapons evocative names.

The last two developments of the weapon were made on the StG44:

- the removal of the butt housing where an instruction notice and a rod for dismantling the hand guard and the cylinder gas cap were placed.

- the removal of the muzzle threading.

In addition, between 1943 and 1945, the finish of certain parts was simplified: the magazine bolt lever was only partly crisscrossed. Some parts, initially bronzed, were parkerized or simply dipped in phosphoric acid.

Initial type firing pin on the right and a late model without a groove on the left.

From left to right: butts in walnut, glued and laminated, beech, and pine.

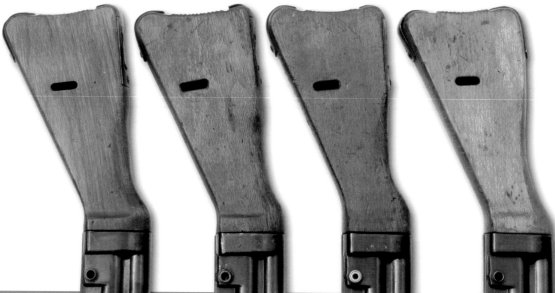

Marking MKb 42 MP43 positioned vertically and horizontally.

Early type magazine pouch with a single flap.

Three types of finish are seen on the magazines, from left to right: parkerized, dipped, and brilliant bronze.

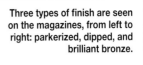

MKb 42 marking.

Code "gqm" on a magazine made by Loch & Hartenberger Metallwarenfabrik.

Markings MP43 and MP44 at right angles.

Accessories

Basic kit. The MP43 was delivered with a sling similar to that on the K.98k carbine, a rubber muzzle cap, an instruction notice, and a disassembly rod as well as a gas cylinder cleaning brush, lodged in the butt, and two magazine pouches containing three magazines each. On one of the magazine pouches there is a pocket containing a guide for feeding magazines with clips of five cartridges. On the other magazine pouch there is a long pocket for housing a small canvas bag containing a firing pin, an extractor, a crossbolt, and a spare extractor spring.

In their initial version, the magazine pouches bore a single flap covering the three magazines. This version was finally abandoned in favor of a more practical one with an individual flap for each of the three magazines. These were made in green, grey-blue, or sand canvas and sometimes having leather reinforcements.

Sights

As we have mentioned earlier, some MP43, MP44, and StG44 are fitted with a welded guide rail on the right of the receiver. This rail enabled the ZF 4 sight to be mounted along with various infra-red optics tried by the *Wehrmacht* at the end of the war.

The "Krummlauf," the famous end piece of the curved barrel which could be mounted on the MP44 to reach blind spots that standard weapons could not.

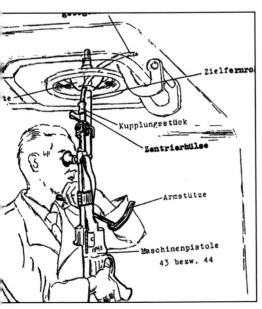

Use of the curved barrel from the inside of a Panzer with an MP44 fitted with a special sight.

MP44 equipped with a guide rail for mounting a ZF4 site. *Musée d'Avranches*

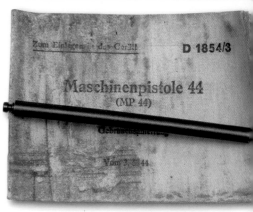

User notice D-1854/3, 03.06.1944 edition entitled "Maschinenpistole 44." On the top left of the cover "*Zum einiegen in das Gerät*" ("place in the weapon").

Second type of magazine pouch with a flap for each compartment. The clip guide is out of the pocket. The canvas has a red weft typical of the makes of the end of the war. *Collection of the Royal Army Museum of Brussels, photo by Marc de Fromont*

Grenade launchers. Unlike the MKb 42 and the MP43/I, which used a specific grenade sleeve which screwed onto the muzzle of the weapon, the MP43 and following models could be equipped with a K.98k carbine grenade thrower. An alidade calibrated in relation to the propulsive capacity of the 43 model cartridge was fixed on the left side of the weapon by a bracket.

Krummlauf. The most original MP44 accessory is without doubt the curved barrel extension, which permitted firing at a 90° angle. This device could be used in street combat or firing from a vehicle, or through a slit in a building. The total weight of the weapon, its curved barrel, and its periscope sight rendered this device sometimes difficult to transport.

Conclusion

The multiple changes of name of this weapon are the origin of a great variety of markings on weapons, magazines, and magazine pouches. This fact is a cause of joy (or despair) for collectors today.

In spite of the decision of the Armaments minister Albert Speer to order the monthly manufacture of 100,000 MP44 and 200 million 7.92 Kurtz cartridges, the MP44 saw its use constantly held up by failings in the supply of ammunition.

In the last months of the war, the depots of the *Wehrmacht* were overflowing with MP44 which could not be distributed due to the lack of enough cartridges. It is doubtless for this reason that many MP44 reached the end of the war totally unused.

The MP44 and various prototypes simplified assault rifles being researched at Mauser, Haenel, and Gustloff in 1945 were seized by the Allied armies highly desirous to test these very promising weapons.

The *Volkspolizei* (VoPo) or the police of the people of East Germany, as well as Czech and Yugoslavian armies, used MP44s that had been abandoned by the *Wehrmacht* in their territory. Several countries of the communist bloc even started production of 7.92 mm Kurtz ammunition, which meant these weapons could finally be used.

After the communist countries in Europe equipped their armies with material subject to the norms imposed by the Warsaw pact, they sold part of the MP44 weapons in their possession to the liberation movements of North Africa. Initially in service in the Algerian National Liberation Army at the end of the Algerian war, these weapons would spread throughout the region and could be encountered in the hands of Palestinian commandos as well as guerillas in the horn of Africa.

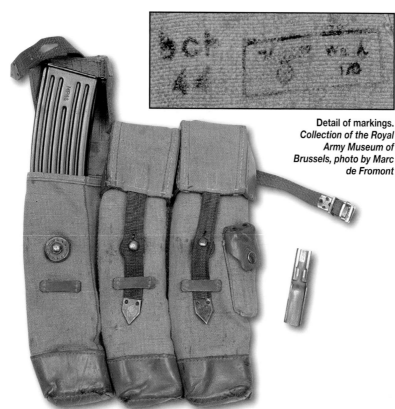

Detail of markings. *Collection of the Royal Army Museum of Brussels, photo by Marc de Fromont*

Use of the guide to fill magazines with the help of 5-round magazine clips.

CLASSIC **GUNS** OF THE **WORLD** SERIES